"That the world may know —"

Road Warrior

Road Warrior

How to Keep Your Faith, Relationships,
and Integrity When Away from Home

Stephen Arterburn
and Sam Gallucci

WATERBROOK
PRESS

Road Warrior
Published by WaterBrook Press
12265 Oracle Boulevard, Suite 200
Colorado Springs, CO 80921
A division of Random House Inc.

ISBN 978-1-4000-7371-9

Library of Congress Cataloging-in-Publication Data
Arterburn, Stephen, 1953–
    Road warrior : how to keep your faith, relationships, and integrity when away from home / Stephen Arterburn and Sam Gallucci. — 1st ed.
        p. cm.
    ISBN 978-1-4000-7371-9
    1. Businesspeople—Religious life. 2. Travel—Religious aspects—Christianity. I. Gallucci, Sam.
II. Title.
    BV4596.B8A78 2007
    248.8'8—dc22

                                                    2007033374

Printed in the United States of America
2008—First Edition

10 9 8 7 6 5 4 3 2 1 0

Special Sales
Most WaterBrook Multnomah books are available in special quantity discounts when purchased in bulk by corporations, organizations, and special interest groups. Custom imprinting or excerpting can also be done to fit special needs. For information, please e-mail SpecialMarkets@ WaterBrookPress.com or call 1-800-603-7051.

To the love of my life, Toni, my wife and best friend.
And to my three sons, Louis, Nick, and Anthony, of whom I am so proud.
Thank You, Lord, for rescuing me.
I love you all.
Sam

To Dale, an international road warrior, a great man, and a great friend.
You are the man.
Steve

Contents

Preface

He was led by the Spirit in the wilderness, where
he was tempted by the devil for forty days.

LUKE 4:1–2, NLT

Whenever you travel away from home, you face unique challenges. Going to a place where you are not known can feel like forging into the wilderness. You can suddenly lose your bearings, your accountability. You can struggle to maintain your integrity and to keep your relationships back home intact.

Ironically, simply keeping things intact isn't what any of us really wants. At our core, we long for true connection and intimacy. We want our relationships to not merely survive but flourish.

If you are one of the 6.5 million frequent travelers across North America, or one of the millions more who love a person who is traveling, then this book is for you. Frequent travelers are vulnerable to temptation and destruction, but there is hope ahead. In the pages to come, we'll show you how to protect the things you hold dear while traveling for work. We'll address some root issues that must be managed proactively while you're on the road. We'll give you some practical tools so you can remain strong and find a healthy, sustainable balance between work, ministry, marriage, and family.

If that sounds like something you want or need, we invite you to keep reading.

—Stephen Arterburn and Sam Gallucci

Welcome to the Pitfalls of Frequent Travel

I (Steve) began hitting the road—or air—when I was still in my twenties. Since then, I have logged more than five million miles, about four million of them on American Airlines. Travel has become a regular part of my life, and virtually every week I find myself on an airplane bound for a new destination.

Early on, I learned that a trip could become an easy escape if I let it. Though the weight of marital problems might sap my energy at home, I could instantly be reenergized as I carried my suitcase out the door (this was before rollers became standard equipment).

But with the world as my playground, temptations lay everywhere. I felt the allure of the road and learned of the disconnection and compartmentalization that can so easily creep into relationships. The road is seductive. It offers a romance all its own, and it's easy to allow it to take hold of you.

How does this dangerous road romance begin?

It's really quite easy. Let's say you're traveling somewhere for business with important and powerful clients. Not only is your identity back home a mystery, but you become a special guest in their eyes. You're the one they go out of their way to make feel welcome. Anonymity and inflated significance—that's a dangerous combination.

Or perhaps you're a long-haul trucker with a load to pull and a check to earn. You've spent all day out on the highway, busting your chops. You're tired;

you're hungry. But the moment you set foot in a motel or truck stop, you're waited on hand and foot. Inside those walls is a sanctuary—it's all about you. You never have to clean up after yourself, wash dirty dishes, discipline your kids, or share the remote. You're the paying customer, and in that kingly environment, you're always right.

In both cases, you learn to develop an attraction for a world quite different from the world you regularly encounter at home. This new world makes you feel consistently important, respected, significant, in control—all the things men (especially) long for. That feeling is highly attractive. The more you feel it, the more you want it.

That's the allure of road romance.

But this new romance is not all it's cracked up to be. Over time, the superficial ways in which you are treated satisfy less and less. You begin to realize a new, gnawing sensation. It may be hard to pinpoint at first, but soon you learn its name.

Loneliness.

It feels painful at first; you wish you were around people who knew you. But over time, in a twisted sort of way, that loneliness can actually begin to feel appealing. As strange as it sounds, left unchecked and unmanaged, loneliness can actually become a romantic pursuit of its own. It becomes something you look forward to, something you learn to not only cope with, but prefer. It is how you live, what you do, who you are, and where you spend the majority of your time.

You're alone and disconnected—and you like it.

I (Sam) was seduced by that strange romance. It nearly destroyed my relationship with my wife and pushed me to the edge of personal disaster for years.

What prevented me from going completely over the falls was a very painful wake-up call (which I will share in the pages ahead) that finally jolted me to my senses. How ironic that my deepest personal failure came at the height of my professional success.

I know I am not alone.

If you travel frequently, or your loved one does, you understand what I'm talking about. We are often perceived as successful, hard-working, and in control of our lives. But we are constantly battling the same problem.

Some of us haven't even stopped long enough to assess the situation, to see that our constant career travel is taking a toll on our lives and on the lives of those we care the most about. It's a horrible trade-off: every career success brings another personal failure.

In the end, what we end up pursuing is that which we have come to hate: *loneliness.* And every mile logged on the road helps dig that pit of despair just a little bit deeper.

Our goal in writing this book is simple: when you travel frequently, you come face to face with forces that can destroy you. We want to prevent that. We've titled this book *Road Warrior* because that's what frequent travelers must become—combatants of destruction, protectors of integrity, guardians of the personal relationships that matter most.

In the next few chapters, we'll address the effects that loneliness can have on a traveler's personal life and relationships. We'll take a look at some of the substitutes we pursue and addictions we find. You'll hear stories from our lives and from the lives of others we know. We'll show you proven strategies to overcome the obstacles that every road warrior faces, and we'll give you the tools to fully protect your personal life and relationships as you travel.

At the end of each chapter, you'll notice a series of questions for reflection. We hope you take advantage of these. They are there to help you sort out the information you read, evaluate your personal situation, and take action to create a battle plan.

No matter how many years you have spent on the road, our hope is that this book stirs you to take action, to invest "face time" in your personal relationships—your spouse, family, and friends. Whether you are single or married, fly in private jets or drive an eighteen-wheeler, you *can* develop balance and fulfillment as you move forward with the rest of your working career.

Quick Guide Summary

PART I: THE CHALLENGE

It's easy to be driven in your job. You want to succeed. But success can wrongly be equated with too much time away from home. When that happens, relationships get damaged, temptation increases, and you begin to pursue loneliness as a way of life.

PART II: THE CONSEQUENCES

When you're away from home too much and setting improper boundaries in your job, you can begin to equate who you are with what you do. Your identity and your job become as one. Soon the people closest to you become distant. You develop short-term memories only, memories created by phone calls and e-mails. These memories don't sustain and protect you in the long run. Too much travel wears you down over time. It may take a severe crisis to cause you to change course.

PART III: THE SOLUTION

Grab the reins of your job today—own it, don't let it own you. Developing five key relationships will help you achieve balance and health in your personal and professional life.

The relationships are:

1. *God.* Go to Him for your ultimate strength.
2. *Spouse.* Consciously work to develop intimacy with your husband or wife.
3. *Children.* Purposefully building into your children's lives creates accountability in your own life. You'll find yourself safeguarding your actions so you can pass on truths to them.
4. *Yourself.* You have to have a life too. Focus on your health—emotional, spiritual, physical, mental, and relational.
5. *Friends.* Develop a trusted group of friends for accountability.

You have more power than you think to create effective boundaries when traveling. Once established and maintained, these boundaries will safeguard your life and personal relationships. If you've erred in this area, take heart. Some adjustment will be required to reorganize your life, but it can be done.

PART I

The Challenge

Driven

The Beginning of a Dangerous Combination

- Business travel is an unavoidable experience in many lines of work. But it isn't the enemy. If God's call for your life involves travel, then thank Him for the opportunity.
- In any line of work, it's easy to fall prey to the trap of being driven, where you push hard to climb the ladder of success. Success sometimes becomes the ultimate goal to be achieved at any cost.
- When you're driven, you can mistakenly equate travel with success. Sometimes a driven person can morph his or her career into a travel lifestyle, always being on the road. Too much travel tends to bring problems into a home and the personal lives involved.
- God calls us to be road warriors, not ladder climbers. God calls us to fight for what matters most—lasting personal relationships.

NOTES FROM SAM'S TRAVELS: PRESENT DAY

It's 4:30 a.m. when the alarm goes off. I turn it off softly so as not to wake up my still-sleeping wife. I shower quickly, suit up, kiss my wife, and head off to the airport to catch a 6:15 flight. No coffee yet; I'm still planning to sleep for another twenty minutes once I board the plane.

I doze through in-flight procedures. The plane takes off as night gives way to sunrise. As the flight attendant brings the coffee down the aisle, I rouse myself awake.

Coffee in hand, I look out the window and watch the sunrise at thirty-five thousand feet. I am inspired by the majesty of it all—the clouds, the red sky, the mountains below. Even with the hum of the engines, it is still quiet, peaceful, even powerful, and I praise God for His glory and majesty.

I also breathe a silent prayer of thanks that God has allowed me to witness this scene this morning. My life could have been so much different than it is today. I'm thankful that His grace reigns strongly in my life—that He is a God of healing, forgiveness, and restoration. I'm thankful that He lifted me up from the depths of despair and set my feet on solid rock.

And from the bottom of my heart, I thank God that I'm ready to attack this new day.

Business travel is an unavoidable experience in many lines of work, including ours, but it isn't the enemy. If God's call for your life involves travel, then thank Him for the opportunity.

I (Sam) still travel for business, though not as much as I used to. But I approach my situation much differently now than I did before. I used to begin each day as a ladder climber. Success for me meant getting to the top. I tackled each task as if my last breath depended on it. But it wasn't long before my fervor led me into one of the darkest periods of my adult life. I realized I needed to change, and now I attack each day as a road warrior—someone who fights for what matters most.

LADDERS LEAD TO PROBLEMS

It's easy to fall prey to the trap of being driven when you travel frequently. It happens to a lot of people, including a longtime friend of mine named Tim. Tim started traveling in the first year of his marriage. He was the top performer in his company and did whatever it took to push the envelope of success. Tim knew the value of face-to-face connections, so he traveled as often as he could to make those connections happen.

After five consecutive years of Tim's intense business travel, his wife, Suzy, asked him for a divorce. They had nothing in common, Suzy said, and she wanted to pursue her own life the same way he had pursued his. Though their young son, Kyle, very much needed both parents at home and engaged, Tim and his wife proceeded with the divorce.

This would surely cause Tim to reevaluate his life, right? Hardly. He continued pursuing his profession with as much zeal as ever. If anything, his schedule increased rather than decreased.

Tim loved his son and worked to stay connected with him, but the year his son turned nine, Tim started to notice a growing distance between them. This was the beginning of his wake-up call.

Tim rearranged his travel schedule to attend as many of his son's baseball games as he could, and Kyle loved having his dad around. A couple of weeks into the season, though, Tim had to go out of town to a national sales meeting. He promised Kyle he would be back in time for his next game.

On the first day of the event, the VP of sales announced that everyone needed to focus solely on business. Anyone caught talking on a cell phone would be fined one hundred dollars. So Tim powered off his phone and didn't think about it until dinner was over and he had spent another several hours at the bar with colleagues. When he turned his phone back on, he heard the startling recorded voice: "You have fifteen unheard messages."

The first message sent fear pulsing through his body: "Tim, it's Suzy. Kyle is in the hospital. Call me immediately!"

Tim instantly phoned his ex-wife without listening to the rest of the messages.

Suzy responded, "You're just calling me now?! I left you over twelve messages! It doesn't surprise me. You've never been there for us—why would you be now?!"

"Suzy! Just tell me what happened to Kyle!"

"He was riding his bike to his baseball practice and got hit by a truck."

"What! Is he okay? Just tell me my son's okay!"

"He was knocked unconscious and was rushed to the emergency room. When I got to him, he was delirious and just kept crying out for you."

"Is he...going to be all right?"

"Well, the doctors said he has a severe concussion and some bleeding in the brain."

"I'm on my way home. I'll be on the next flight out and get there as soon as I can."

Tim found a red-eye flight heading back in the direction of his son, and on the way to the airport, he listened to the other messages.

The second message came through: "Tim, call me please! This is Suzy. It's an emergency!"

The third message came through: "Tim, you have got to call me. Kyle is in really bad shape. He's calling out for you. Please pick up the phone. He needs you right now, and so do I." In the background he could hear his son's voice, *"Daddy! Daddy! Daddy!"*

That was the message he needed to hear. If any event could provide the moment of clarity he needed, that was it. Tim shook his head. How had his life become reduced to airplanes, cabs, and hotels, where a mere snippet of conversation was all the time he spent with his family in an entire day?

He realized how absurd his life had become, how lonely he was. Anger flashed toward his boss and his company—the demands of work just never seemed to stop. He asked himself, *What in the world have I been doing all these years?* With his head in his hands, Tim began to weep, "My son, my son…"

Thankfully, Tim's son later made a full recovery. Tim and his wife aren't together today, but Tim has made some significant changes in his priorities since that powerful moment of truth.

WHEN YOU BECOME DRIVEN

Tim's story raises a few questions for all of us: What does it take for us to notice how imbalanced our lives have become? How bad does it have to get? What horrible thing needs to happen to get our attention and motivate us to change?

Over the years, I often wondered how it was that my own career developed into a full-time travel lifestyle. In the end, I wasn't making occasional trips out of town; I was making consistent, weekly treks far away from home.

I started my career with a large technology company. That first year on the job I was required to travel for twenty weeks of training. I was very anxious to succeed and quickly developed a keen sense of business competition. My pursuit and focus were to be the absolute best at what I did—the number one sales representative. I wanted to accomplish more than anyone in my company had ever accomplished. Within the same period of time, I met the woman of my dreams and got married. I had launched both a career and a marriage, and the postcollege phase of my life began to unfold as I always dreamed it would.

Initially, I felt excitement and adventure as I visited places I had never been before. I imagined myself like the early explorers who sailed in, stayed a few days while conducting business, and then breezed out to the next far-off port. I met people from all over the country and came face to face with a multitude of exciting subcultures within America. After I had been in my job a few years, my travel experiences began to take me all over the world.

It sounds a lot more glamorous than it was. It was not until I could answer the question about *why* I was traveling so much that I could begin to understand what to do to overcome my lonely pursuits.

Stop and think for a moment about what makes a person become *driven.* Do you think you're driven? What does that look like?

Is it a personality trait?

Is it a sense of responsibility to provide?

Is it a desire for material things—cars, houses, or fancy suits?

Is it a sense of competition?

Is it insecurity—will you be a success only if you *win*?

Is it duty—do you have to succeed for some noble cause?

I believe people become driven for a variety of reasons. Sometimes it's just the way you are, but most often it's what you choose to become. It doesn't really matter. Whatever motivates you in the beginning of your career can easily become a driving force for your entire life. Often, the longer you live as a driven person, the more you'll convince yourself you're doing it for the good of your family.

Being driven has a way of blinding you to what's truly important in life. You become driven to *succeed,* and success becomes the end goal, regardless of what success actually looks or feels like. That quest for success will then override any and all relationships that matter most—your spouse, your kids, your friends. All begin to suffer under the driving force of success.

What does a driven person look like? Take this quick inventory to see if any of these traits fit your lifestyle. Answer "yes," "no," or "sometimes" to the following questions:

Yes	Sometimes	No	
			You're highly involved with your career. Some would call you "obsessed."
			You have a high desire to be financially well off.
			You desire success at every level of your work.
			Your prime concern is satisfying whoever is in authority over you—your boss or supervisor.
			Your main goals involve developing relationships with customers, suppliers, and partners involved in your work.
			Most of your energy revolves around key people associated with your work.
			Your (not-so-hidden) motto is "work at any cost."
			Family time fits into work time—not the other way around.
			You're eager to travel whenever work calls for it.
			Work is the consuming fire within you.

We won't score you on any of these questions; they're just for your reflection. But chances are good that if you answered "yes" or "sometimes" to the majority of those questions, you're on some risky ground with regard to your motivations while away from home.

EXAMINING YOUR BUSINESS MODEL

I know that in my frantic efforts to succeed in my own life, I failed in the one area that was most important to me: the relationships with my family. As a business traveler I lived a hypocritical life. I understood the value of relationships for business purposes, but my investment in them was disproportionate to their true long-term value in my personal life.

Sales 101 will tell you that it takes face time to develop relationships with customers, suppliers, and partners. That's just good business. It's why I used to get on airplane after airplane. Yet for some reason, I expected that everything on the home front would be just fine when I walked through the door, even though I didn't invest any time there to ensure it would be. Where was the face time with my spouse, kids, friends, or extended family members?

Think of what you know to be true in the business world. If you're a driven person and typically don't spend much time at home, reverse the tables for a minute. Imagine you spent the same amount of time in your job as you spend at home. How successful at your job would you be then? If you thought that simply using the phone would be good enough, would you still be as successful?

No. You travel to meet people because you know that in any face-to-face meeting, you'll make better progress in developing the relationship and landing or keeping the sale. You know that it requires face time to develop trust, friendship, and confidence with others.

So here's the hard question: if you know this to be true in a business model, how can an occasional phone call to your spouse and kids possibly be enough to develop, nurture, and sustain these highly important personal relationships?

Whenever you invest time in your personal relationships, you begin to see a positive return. Your marriage improves. Your children are more secure. You begin to feel more supported and encouraged. But the pursuit of loneliness starts when you begin to fill your time with substitutes instead of real personal relationships.

It's been said that a driven man is a blind man. I agree. It becomes very hard to see the big picture when you're driven. That certainly describes my life. I had crafted a million justifications for what I was doing; it was always about the next sale, the next contact, the next trip, the next "success."

Sure, there were warnings along the way from my wife and friends. Others knew all my traveling was having a negative effect on the people who mattered most to me. But I always had answers for them: "This is just what I do" or "This is all I know" or "I'm trying to make a living for us" or "Don't you think this is hard for me too?" I grew frustrated. After all, anyone could see the results of all my hard labor. We had a fancy house in a great neighborhood, new cars, nice stuff, and exotic vacations, and the kids went to the best schools. Good grief, what more do you want?!

I remember many conversations with my wife about the effects of my travel. After a while I started to get mad at her for complaining all the time. I thought my wife had lost her perspective on the importance of my career. I knew a lot of people who traveled for work. I was convinced that being away all the time was just the way it had to be. It is unbelievable to me now, but that is what I thought she was doing—complaining. I learned later that she and the kids were actually *starving* for my time and love.

WHAT DRIVES YOU?

This is a common cycle. I (Steve) had rarely traveled while I was growing up, so when I was given a territory (one-half of the United States), a credit card, and an expense account, I saw it as a great privilege and an opportunity to see the world. What I did not see was that traveling was the perfect excuse for what I call an avoidant personality—I avoided the personalities that needed me most.

It was not until years into my career that a wise friend advised me that whenever frequency of travel increases, problems in marriage are soon to follow. But I was blind to that. The greater the problems at home, the more reasons I found to be gone.

Is that your story too? Each time you head out the door, ask yourself if you are truly leaving to go to work…or leaving to escape conflict or pain in your home life.

In my specific job, I had some discretion as to when I could travel, but you may not be like me. You fly in the plane or drive the truck not because you want to leave but because it is your life. If so, you have to work twice as hard to stay connected, to eradicate the feelings of abandonment that may exist back home.

Being driven is not wrong. Driven people get things done and typically do the things that change the world. But sometimes they are so driven they never stop to look at the motives or desires behind the drive.

Too often people work for years in an area they hate because they are too afraid to stop and ask why they are doing it. Is it out of a love for something or in reaction to a lack of love? Is it an attempt to attain something or to compensate for something that isn't there? Is it fueled by a healthy perspective on life or by a wound that no accomplishment will ever heal?

If you never stop to evaluate what you are doing and why, you may find yourself feeling like a failure no matter how strong your success. This is the beginning of a pursuit of loneliness; it is the genesis of a lifestyle that will soon be marked by emptiness.

So again I ask, what is it that drives you? Where did this drive start for you in a life now marked by constant travel? Was it a career that somehow convinced you that travel was the only way to achieve your goals? Could it have been the need to fill some inner void? It's so easy to keep on traveling while giving little thought to the consequences of our actions.

It's our drivenness that starts us down the path of loneliness. And it's loneliness that can, in many cases, push us toward a crisis of personal and profes-sional destruction.

Stop before it's too late. Stop and take stock of your life. Put some serious thought into what drives you. Know your goals and discuss them with the people who are closest to you. Then ask yourself if reaching those goals is what's truly important—to you and the ones you love.

Questions to Ponder

1. In your most honest moments, what would you say drives you? How does that make you feel?
2. How driven does your spouse or best friend say you are? Do you agree? What do you think of his or her perspective?
3. How often do you make decisions based on what drives you? How often do you evaluate what drives you within the frame-work of your entire life? Take some time to do that now. Is there anything that you might be paying too much attention to compared with the amount of time you spend with your friends and family?

2

Success

A Word with More than One Definition

- Having a job is a good thing. God calls us to be productive, responsible people. But it's possible to glean *too much* importance from a job. A job is important, but it's not *everything*. Your true identity is not defined by what you do.
- It's easy to equate success with traveling. Your company's decision to send you on a trip communicates trust to you. You're the man (or woman) to get the job done. The more you travel, the more successful you must be. Right?
- Wrong. Success can become an evil master if your personal life suffers. When this happens, you begin to travel in the pursuit of loneliness.
- Success can actually become an addiction. The more you travel, the more successful you think you are. So you feel the need to travel more to keep up with the feeling of being valued.

It's 7:00 a.m. local time (4:00 a.m. body-clock time) when the phone rings. Ah, yes, the wake-up call. I answer and hang up. Within minutes, coffee arrives at the door. After coffee I shower, iron my shirt, get dressed, and head out the door and down to breakfast.

I look over my day's list of meetings and review how I will approach each one. I am ready. This is my routine. I am focused on the job at hand. I jump into the rental car and head off to the first call. There's a huge part of work I enjoy. I'm good at this. I feel good when I work hard. When the day is over, I look back and know that things went well.

Busy. Important. Capable. Trusted. Having those feelings at work is not wrong. God created us to be productive—to reflect His glory in our work and lives. Even Adam, the first human created, was given a job in the Garden of Eden. His task was not just to name the animals but to care for the garden and do whatever was required to make it flourish. It's reasonable to assume that Adam took the animal-naming job to heart.

But for Adam and for us, there is a lesson that it's also possible to glean *too much* importance from a job. A job is important, but it's not *everything*. Your true identity is not the same as what you do.

In my (Sam's) early years on the job, it was easy to think of myself as more important than I really was. The temptation of pride is ever present. I think a lot of people fall into that trap, including Bill, a businessman I met on a plane recently.

Bill told me a revealing and embarrassing story about himself. A few months ago, Bill was at the end of a long day of meetings in Denver. He jumped into his rented Cadillac and drove back to the airport. On the way, he left several voice-mail messages confirming his next day's appointments. Everything seemed to be going well; he was having another successful week on the road. The trip back to the airport was perfectly coordinated to ensure enough time to turn in the rental car and check in for the flight.

Bill had the highest status membership at the rental car company, which meant no waiting to check in the car. He was a platinum member of the airline club, so no waiting to check in for the flight, either. Bill hated waiting, and on most trips he didn't have to.

But this night in Denver was not one of those nights. The weather changed rapidly. Soon flights had to be delayed. Passengers began piling up, and even with his frequent-flyer bonus, Bill was forced to stand in line. He tapped his foot. He glanced at his watch. He craned his neck to check on the gate agent. *Why is she taking so long?!*

Then came the dreaded announcement: "Attention, please. Flight 224, service to Atlanta, has been canceled. Everyone standing in line will be re-booked on the next available flight."

The groans from the other passengers were audible.

Bill snapped. He pushed his way to the front of the line, slapped his ticket down on the counter and said, "I *must* be on the next flight, and I *must* be in *first class!*"

"I'll be happy to assist you," the agent said, "but I've got to help these folks first. Then I'm sure we'll be able to work something out for you."

Bill raged. "I can't wait!" he bellowed. "Do you have any idea *who I am?*"

Without hesitating, the gate agent smiled and calmly reached for her public-address microphone. "May I have your attention, please?" her voice sounded throughout the terminal. "We have a passenger here at gate 17 *who does not know who he is.* If anyone knows this man, please come to gate 17." The agent then quietly set her microphone down and returned to helping other passengers.

AH, THE SWEET SMELL OF...

Success can breed a sense of entitlement, and Bill is the first to admit he thought the world revolved around him. While this example may seem extreme, forms of this type of thinking emerge in everyday life more than we realize. When a successful traveling businessman's entire feeling of self-worth is based on how well he performs for the company, almost anything seems feasible as he strives to meet his goals.

He may even think he's the most important passenger on an airplane.

Success can mean different things to different people. It can mean that someone has achieved a certain level in a company. Or it can mean a person has achieved a certain goal that was set for him, such as a sales quota, a new business relationship, or a long-term contract with money and business directed into the company.

It's easy to equate success with traveling. Somehow, they seem to feed off each other. Your company's decision to send you on a trip communicates trust. You're the man (or the woman) to get the job done. The drones are back at their desks working, but you—you've got what it takes to be out in the field. The more you travel, the more successful you must be. Right?

My definition of success developed in the first year of my career when I achieved or exceeded literally *all* of the objectives set for me. I traveled extensively, and each time I returned from a trip, I would receive great encouragement from my superiors to "keep up the good work."

Little by little, I started to associate my self-worth with the amount of time I was devoting to travel. I began to see a connection between being on the road to meet clients regularly and my success in business. It was a subtle connection, but I found that the more time I spent cultivating relationships with customers, partners, and suppliers, the more money I made. The more money I made, the more awards and positive feedback I received from my boss and the rest of the executive team. The more awards and accolades I received, the better I felt about myself. The lines all blurred for me between success, self-worth, and travel. It was a vicious cycle. I began to replace true love and affection from those who truly cared for me with the pseudolove and affection of those at work who only cared about my performance.

I remember calling my wife once on her birthday. My side of the conversation went something like this:

> Happy birthday, honey! How was your party? I am so sorry I missed it, but we'll celebrate when I get home this weekend…
>
> Yes, I know I have missed a few things, but I had no choice this time. My boss called, and I had to go to this meeting. He needed me…
>
> Oh, guess what? I had a great meeting and a really successful day. My boss can't stop talking to everyone about how well I did. He's so thankful I was there for him.

It was my wife's birthday, and all I could talk about was how great I was doing at work.

MARRIED IN NAME ONLY

If you believe that production at work will ever bring love, you are sorely mistaken. In this system, "love" must be earned, so you have to work hard for it. Once the production falls off—and it will—then the love is removed. And along the way you'll distance yourself from those closest to you.

Remember the last time you came home and couldn't understand why your spouse didn't respond to you when you reached for him or her? You probably became frustrated because you had convinced yourself that the only reason you were out working so hard was for your spouse and family. Yet you still didn't get the support and respect you craved when you returned home. Why is that?

The truth is that life at home is hard. Once you fall into the cycle, it's just easier to stay away. Whether we verbalize it or not, we all want to get back on the road as soon as possible. We long for the peace and quiet of being alone. Compared to the boisterous environment of kids and spouses and noise and dirty dishes, a hotel room can feel like heaven.

But those of us who hit the road are not the only ones who feel this way. And while we breathe a sigh of relief in the cab ride to catch the next flight out of town, our spouses are left to manage by themselves as best they can.

Most spouses left in this situation will begin to respond in one of two ways. Either they'll become indifferent and cease to contribute romance and excitement to the marriage, or they'll become hostile and offer resistance, resentment, and bitterness toward you every time you leave and every time you return home.

In order to cope, spouses learn to become independent of each other. They develop separate lives that only come together around common goals, such as finances or children. They become the "married divorced" as their relationship gradually moves more toward a domestic partnership.

Once this happens—moving from a *relationship* to a *partnership*—spouses actually lose their ability to distinguish between the two modes of operation. At that point, all bets are off. The vows, rules, and parameters that once held the marriage together begin to crumble. Here destruction looms. And sadly, when the destruction finally comes, it can in many cases be permanent.

FARTHER DOWN THE RABBIT HOLE

But there are warning signs along the way. When I reached this point in my own marriage, I began to suffer from a nagging sense of loneliness that I couldn't quite pinpoint. I knew something was wrong, but I quickly learned to live with the feeling, as if it were a low-grade fever. Why?

I was successful in my work, and every time I got back on the road, I would feel better about myself for a little while. I was like a junkie looking for just one more fix. The deeper I dove into the snare of success, the more I had to travel to keep up the feeling of being valued. An addiction was setting in, which involved at least three components:

- Success at work was replacing *intimacy* in my relationships.
- Success at work was replacing *depth of living* in my personal life.
- Success at work was replacing all the *true loves* of my life.

And in the absence of love, once those relationships had been severed, I began to experience an awful and painful emotional consequence that led me farther down the path of destruction. The longer my "success" ran, the longer I delayed developing relationships that could truly fulfill me. A void in my heart had begun to develop.

I had become so proficient in receiving love based on what I did that I forgot how to receive love based on just being me. What's more, I forgot how to give love to others for simply being themselves. I forgot how to think about others first. It's amazing that we can go so long and so fast and work so hard without developing true relationships. Instead, what we *do* develop is a relationship with loneliness. For most of us, it doesn't take long to experience the accumulated true cost of our daily choices.

A good friend of mine reached this place. He had lived in the fast track for too long, and once he discovered his success was gone, he realized just how little he had invested in other areas of his life. He had huge pension and 401(k) plans all tied up with a nice, neat bow, but he was bankrupt in his relationships, in himself, and in the faith he once nurtured.

So what did he do? Sadly, he threw himself into another job where success required travel. In the end, the addiction he had formed was all he had to fall back on.

The landscape of travel is littered with people who reached the end of their ropes and thought they were starting over but were in reality simply reentering their cycle of loneliness at another point.

There are many benefits to being successful in a career, but success can become an evil master if we let it take us away from the ones we love. You see, God has designed us to be in relationship with other people and with Him. We long for the fulfillment that comes from developing and maturing close, intimate relationships that are based not on what we do but on who we are.

But there is hope that we can overcome our cycle of loneliness and return to the life God designed us for. If we can learn to make connections and build relationships for business purposes on the road, then we can surely do so where it matters most—in the home. We can still let God into our hearts and ask Him to help us redefine what it means to be a success.

Questions to Ponder

1. Is every trip you take totally necessary for your success? Why or why not?
2. List some of the professional accomplishments you have experienced while traveling for work. How long did the feelings of accomplishment last?
3. To what degree has your success started to cut you off from others? What things in your life is the pursuit of success starting to take the place of? How does that make you feel?

3

Don't Think—Just Do

What Happens When We Stop Asking Why

- When you're a driven person and start to experience success, you tend to go on autopilot with travel. Out-of-town travel gets lumped into the same category as going to the store. It simply *has* to be done.

- When too much travel is a pattern in your life, you seldom consider the rightness or wrongness of a trip. Instead, you focus on the activities that must be executed once you arrive. Maybe in your early days you wonder about the impact of a trip on your family. But as time goes on, you stop thinking those thoughts. What matters then is the outcome of the mission that lies ahead. You've accepted the fact that you *must* travel, so you don't think—*you just do*!

- Too much travel can fill you with a deep sense of emptiness. As the close ties in your life begin to be loosened and severed, you lose your bearings.

- When you begin to schedule trips where little business is accomplished, you're in trouble. You've gotten to the point where you don't even try to reschedule meetings when they conflict with your personal life. You're running headlong in pursuit of loneliness.

It's 10:00 a.m. and I am in my office at home. The phone rings and its one of my customers in New York. "Yes, I can meet you any time... Later this week?... Sure, I'll be there." I hang up the phone and arrange travel plans. I need to get back on the road.

Let's see...with only one appointment scheduled, where else should I go and who else can I see while I'm there?

A couple more phone calls and now I have a second day partially scheduled. I'll need to squeeze one more meeting in, maybe one more appointment to fill in each day.

I make a few more calls. I am sure I can make this happen, but for now I confirm the travel plans I have made. Okay, New York—here I come! Another trip planned means another opportunity for success. Great!

Now that the trip is scheduled, I have to rearrange my personal schedule. But that shouldn't be a problem. My wife, well, she'll just have to handle these details. After all, business is calling...

P rogress. Momentum. Opportunity. These were all words I (Sam) lived by when I scheduled each new business trip. For years I was on auto-pilot in the fast lane. Many weeks I had planned to be home were unexpectedly rearranged to make room for one-day or overnight trips. I was convinced that these "short" trips did not count in my overall time away, but that was simply not the case.

My wife had heard the story many times before—"It's just a quick trip; I'll be home soon; I won't miss anything"—but she knew the truth. Whenever I came to tell her I needed to rearrange our personal schedule for another trip, she would turn away with an almost palpable indifference to me and return to her business of running the household.

But I never stayed. Again and again, I left.

I remember one trip in particular. I had promised Toni it would be a quick one. For me, it was just business as usual. I received my wake-up call, had coffee, showered, went to breakfast alone, then got ready for another day of work. But for some reason I had only scheduled one meeting that day. When I came back it was still early afternoon. I sat in my hotel room thinking, *Did I really have to come out here this week? Could I possibly have kept this trip to a one-day event rather than an overnighter?*

That night I lay in my hotel room wondering what was happening at home and how my kids were ending their evening. I wondered what their morning would be like the next day—simple things, like if they were getting ready for school or the type of mood they would wake up with or what they would eat for breakfast.

For one stark moment an emptiness filled me like never before.

But then I stopped and thought, *I am providing for my family... This is okay... This is what I do... Everything will be all right...*

And the moment was gone.

"I MUST GO"

When you're a driven person and start to experience success, you tend to go on autopilot with travel. Out-of-town travel gets lumped into the same category as going to the store. It simply *must* be done.

You seldom consider the rightness or wrongness of the trip. Instead, you focus on the activities that must be executed once you arrive. Maybe in your early days you wonder about the impact of the trip on your family. But as time goes on, you stop thinking those thoughts. What matters is the outcome of the mission. You've accepted the fact that you *must* travel, so you don't think—*you just do*!

When you stop consciously considering the absolute need for these trips, you stop thinking about the impact on your family, spouse, and children, and on your mental or physical state of being. Another trip becomes just something that you do—it's what you put on your calendar because that's what always goes there. The worst part is when you believe you can somehow lead a normal and healthy personal life, even when you travel every five out of seven days.

That's where I was. I had fooled myself into believing travel would have little impact on my life, even while I was spending more and more time away.

Being away from home felt so normal after a while. In the early days I scheduled my meetings as tightly as I could, but as the years went on, I found myself away from home with larger and larger blocks of time on my hands. Somehow the urgency to come home—of needing to return to my wife and family—simply wasn't there anymore.

And the allure of travel diminished also. After a while, the cities all started to look the same. Hotel chains. Rental car companies. Everything was the same, and it became less and less important where I was. I'd often have to remind myself what city I was in and why I was even there. I was just away—and away was normal.

After all those years of travel, the details of the places I had been blurred in my mind. The people I met were no different from those I had met the week before—they began to lose their individual identities. Have you ever seen time-lapse photography of a man sitting in an airport while all the people pass him by? The man remains still—unchanged by all the activity around him—but the faces and the colors of the clothes of all the people passing by run together. You can't tell one from another. Well, that man was me, and I hated it.

THE EFFECTS OF FREQUENCY

Have you reached a place like that in your travels?

The truth is, frequent travel isn't what it's cracked up to be. Regular business trips are lonely times. You always seem to be talking with someone you don't really know and about things you don't really care about. Life on the road is shallow.

The funny thing is that most of the time the people you meet are in the same boat you're in. So for a brief period they seem interested, and so do you. But as soon as you leave that city, you start all over again. It's the same conversation with the same outcome—loneliness.

Why is that? It's because you are not being fulfilled in your primary relationships. The more you travel, the more loneliness is able to take hold. The longer you're away from those who matter most, the bigger that hole in your life begins to feel. So why do we keep doing it? Because we have stopped thinking and are just going through the motions. It's what we're used to, and so it's where we feel comfortable.

What's the path that leads to this state?

It's *frequency.*

Most people can handle one or two trips away from home per year without a problem. One or two trips per month are probably okay too.

But the further you push that envelope, the more blurred those lines will become.

Different jobs will require different things from you. And being away from home is unavoidable in some jobs. But it's not always unavoidable. Most jobs allow you some discretion in the number of trips you schedule. But how do you know when you've crossed the line? When you begin taking trips that accomplish very little business, it's time to reevaluate.

Maybe someone in authority asked you to go, or maybe you just had the uncontrollable urge to get on the road. Regardless of the reason, it's clear that travel has taken charge. You can't say no to that next trip. You can't say no to that next meeting. You have gotten to the point where you don't even try to reschedule events when they conflict with your personal life. And when your spouse challenges you, you flatly and sometimes even vehemently deny that work controls you.

But it does. You are a slave to your job and a slave to travel. Why? Because you have lost your ability to balance your health and personal relationships with your career. When this happens, every part of your life suffers—even your business life.

But there is hope. You have the power to make the decisions you need to. Take some time right now to do the hard work of examining your life. Decide now what kind of success you'd like to pursue. If you're operating in a "don't think—just do" mode, there's still time to switch gears and regain a life of balance.

Questions to Ponder

1. Have you ever scheduled trips before you had reason to? Or do you schedule trips without a complete itinerary, knowing you'll take advantage of the extra time away? Why or why not?
2. Why do you get the urge to travel for work? What amount of influence do you have over the amount of time you spend traveling?
3. What motivates you to keep traveling? When is the last time you sat down and really examined the motives that drive you? Take some time to do that now.

PART II

The Consequences

4

A Lonesome Identity

A Life of Travel Is a Life on Hold

- Being alone isn't wrong. Often Christ withdrew from the masses of people and spent time in prayer and solitude. But too much time alone can become unhealthy. It's unhealthy when you no longer seek time alone for the sake of recharging your batteries but instead seek it as a means of escape.
- Left unchecked and unmanaged, this type of unhealthy behavior can consume your identity. Being alone becomes how you live, what you do, who you are, and where you spend the majority of your time. Like it or not, being alone has become a pseudoromantic attraction for you, and you have entered fully into your pursuit of loneliness.
- Too much travel can cause you to lose your sense of self and will wreak havoc on your character. It can make you impatient, demanding, self-absorbed, and shallow. You can become accustomed to having things your own way.

NOTES FROM SAM'S TRAVELS: IN THE PAST

On the road, days are filled with meetings. I'm usually worn out as evening approaches, and this trip is no exception. I'm really ready for some downtime.

As I drive back to my hotel, I start to anticipate the evening ahead. I'm staying at a hotel I've stayed at before, so I ponder what will greet me when I arrive at my home away from home. I know the room will be quiet and comfortable—just the way I like it. I'll go out to my favorite restaurant for a meal or maybe order room service in. Everything will be peaceful and comforting.

I'm excited about the chance to finally be alone again. I can hear the solitude calling my name. With no other person around, I will be able to jump into my next novel or maybe watch a good movie. This really is my time, which I can seldom find anywhere else.

B eing alone isn't wrong. Jesus often withdrew from the masses of people to spend time in prayer and solitude. But too much time alone can become unhealthy for a person. It's unhealthy when you no longer seek time alone for the sake of recharging batteries but instead seek it as a means of escape.

Left unchecked and unmanaged, this type of unhealthy behavior can become part of your identity. Being alone becomes how you live, what you do, who you are, and where you spend the majority of your time. It can even become a pseudoromantic attraction and send you further along in your pursuit of loneliness.

A LIFE ON HOLD

I (Sam) followed this attraction for several years, and I know others have followed the same dangerous path. For example, here is the story of my friend Andrew, who found himself in a similar predicament.

Andrew told me about going to a wedding recently and having a conversation with the groom that finally made him stop and think. He had only wanted to congratulate Joe on his beautiful wedding and wish him luck in the future with his new wife, but some of Joe's questions caught him off guard.

"What about you? What are you doing these days? Last I heard you left your apartment in Atlanta and have all your stuff in storage. Are you ever going to settle down?"

You see, Andrew didn't really have any one place to call home anymore. He just went wherever work sent him. Joe couldn't believe it. "So you're just living out of a suitcase? Andrew, are you crazy?"

Crazy? The thought had never occurred to Andrew. He just traveled a lot. That was normal, wasn't it? A dangerous pattern of loneliness had slowly infiltrated Andrew's life without his knowing. He hadn't realized how skewed his life had become until the blinders came off that day at the wedding.

Everything had started normal enough. Andrew graduated from college, found a job he liked, and began his career. For the first ten years, work dominated much of his life. Andrew kept up an extensive business travel schedule and saved as much money as possible.

One by one, all of his college friends got married. Andrew didn't see them much anymore anyway. He was always away on business. He had lots of friends—acquaintances, really. It didn't bother him much to sever ties. His boss was always happy with his performance. More travel meant more perks. It only seemed prudent to get rid of his apartment and just live from one trip to the next. He was never at his apartment anyway.

Hearing Joe's comment at the wedding, Andrew began to suspect for the first time that something wasn't right. His drive for success had cost him a life outside of work. He had defined his life by travel, and in the end, travel was all he had. He had no home, no friends, no close ties with family members. He was alone, desperately alone.

WHO ARE YOU ANYWAY?

Letting your life be defined by travel is so easy to do. If traveling is all you do, that's all you have. Your life can become one dimensional, and it will get harder and harder to adjust back to normal every time you come home. At some point you might even become like Andrew—with nothing left to come home to.

I remember one incident with an associate named Alan. We had just spent a long day away on a business trip. It was dinnertime, and Alan and I made casual conversation. He wanted to know a little more about me and asked what I liked to do in my spare time.

"Well, I love skiing and hiking, and I love good jazz."

"That's great, Sam. How long has it been since you've been hiking?"

"Well, I guess it's been a while. I can't actually say. Maybe five years. Maybe longer."

"How about jazz? Which artists do you like the most?

"Uh…my favorites are…uh…hmm…"

"And skiing?"

"Well, actually, I haven't done that in years, either."

As I sat there, I realized the truth—I had no hobbies. No real ones anyway. I claimed I had hobbies, but I never participated in any of them. My hiking boots had not been worn in years. I didn't even exercise anymore. I certainly hadn't been skiing any time recently. I hadn't added one album to my jazz collection since the late eighties.

What did I like to do? The more I thought about it, the more I realized I had no idea. I came to the conclusion that I really didn't know myself very well. My identity was wrapped up in travel—it was all I had time for and all I *made* time for. Travel was not only *what I did*, it had become the sum total of *who I was*.

Too much travel can do this. It can make you lose your sense of self. When you put your life on hold while you go away to make a living, all the foundations in your life remain foundations only. You never build anything. You never build up the real relationships that form the home you live in. That was certainly my story. The bulk of my personal time was spent in hotel rooms. I was constantly surrounded by complete strangers and the few people who worked weekly with me. The entire contents of my real world were what I lugged around in my suitcase.

Too much travel wreaked havoc on my character. Travel made me more impatient, more demanding, more self-absorbed, and more shallow. I became conditioned to expect and demand service when I was on the road. (And I would be the first to let businesses know when I did not get it.) Couple this with the growing intensity of my work schedule, and who I was becoming was neither my true identity nor who I remotely wanted to be. One day I woke up and did not know the answer to the question, *Who am I?*

Does any of this ring a bell?

I have seen many travelers become so burned out, so out of gas, that they go into depression. Others get divorced, and the few who are still together with their spouses usually lead very independent lives.

Each day on the road put the rest of my life on hold because I did not have a consistent enough schedule to build on my personal character. I was a long way from being a person of balance. I had developed a one-dimensional life.

If you have just started traveling for work, the imbalance may not be obvious to you. But time and your schedule will soon make it very clear if you do not stop long enough to count the cost of your life.

CONSIDER YOUR FUTURE

Could it be time to start building on the other areas of your life? Or to rebuild some of the areas and personal relationships that have fallen into disrepair because of your traveling lifestyle? Could it be time to build a life without addictions, a life of new memories and renewed purpose?

Well, I have good news and bad news for you. The bad news is that you have lost time. You cannot change your past. Lost time with your spouse or your children cannot be regained. All those missed birthdays and ball games cannot be redone. But the good news is that it's not too late to change your future. This may sound simplistic, but it is very important to note so that you can have hope.

In the depths of my (Steve's) despair, I went to see a pastoral counselor, Milan Yerkovich. In the first session he heard how my ex-wife betrayed me and how crushed I was. He talked for a few minutes, and then he said something that caused my dark-circled, tear-filled eyes to look up: "I can help you get your life back."

I had lost *me*. I had become something or someone else. With the hope of finding me again, I began to work with my counselor. He was right. He could help. And he did. You can find yourself too. Milan Yerkovich wrote a book with his wife, Kay, titled *How We Love,* and if you want help finding your way back, this book is a good place to start.

Is this your story too? With too much travel in your life, it can be easy to lose your identity. Take some time to honestly examine your life today. Be willing to do the necessary work to reorder your priorities and get on the path to living a balanced life.

Questions to Ponder

1. What do you like to do for recreation? When is the last time you really pursued these interests? What can you do to involve your loved ones in the things you enjoy?

2. What other types of things have you put on hold for your career? Time with your children? Family vacations? Home improvements? Gardening? How does this make you feel?

3. What can you do now to start developing other parts of your life?

5

Severed Relationships

Relationships Define Our Lives

- Too much travel adversely affects close relationships. The scary part is, you may not really know the full impact of the time you spend away from your family until years later.
- Close, personal relationships are an absolute in life. You cannot survive without them. No investment in business relationships will bring results as important as the result of your investment in personal relationships.
- True, real, fulfilling, long-lasting, and intimate relationships can only be developed face to face. Relationships require your physical presence.
- Intimate relationships happen from special moments that can seldom be planned in advance. You might have heard the old adage: It's not quantity time that matters; it's quality time. But really, that's a partial truth. Quality time matters, but quality time can only happen when plenty of quantity time is available.

NOTES FROM SAM'S TRAVELS: IN THE PAST

It's Friday night. I managed to get home early in time to see the kids and help them get to bed.

Now with the kids asleep, I reach for my wife. She knows the look in my eyes. She knows what I want. I have been away for the week and I need some physical intimacy, but she pulls away. I get angry and we plunge into another argument. I remind her that it has been over ten days since we have been close.

"No, it hasn't," she says. "It has only been three days. The other seven days don't count because you were not here. All you want is sex. What about us?"

"Honey, I called you every night when I was away," I say. "Doesn't that count for something?"

"No, it does not count," she says. "Can't we ever just spend time together without sex? This is the only time I have your full attention."

A big argument ensues followed by a rough night of sleep.

Welcome home.

Travel adversely affects close relationships. There is no way around it. The scary part is that you may not really know the full impact of the time you spend away from your family until years later.

This is how it went with Peter, a dedicated, hard-working family man. Peter had spent about fifteen years traveling with what appeared to be no negative effects on his family relationships. He had two daughters, three years apart. The girls seemed to grow up well.

But Peter and his wife, Janie, started to notice a change in their teenage daughter, Lilly, right around her fifteenth birthday. She started wearing a lot of dark things—dark eyeliner, dark jeans, dark shirts, dark jackets—and hanging out with kids who concerned her parents.

Lilly began spending most of her time in her room and refused to hang out with her family in the evenings. Whenever Peter came home from a business trip, Lilly would brush off his suggestions of spending any time together.

He would ask about how she was doing and what was going on in her life, but she only gave one-word answers. "Fine." "No." "Nothing."

As that year progressed, Lilly's attitude and actions toward her dad became even more negative and distant. Peter wondered if it was just a phase.

One day he came home and Janie met him in the driveway. She was frantic. "Pete, Lilly's left with Josh! She left a note saying she's gone for good. I called her, but she's not answering her cell. I called several of her friends, and no one has heard from her."

Josh was a big concern for them. He was twenty-two, was rumored to be using drugs, and seemed to have very little motivation to do anything in life other than hang around their daughter. That night, all Peter and Janie could do was pray. At 2:00 a.m. the phone rang. Janie picked up the receiver.

"Hello? Mom? This is Lilly."

"Lilly, we are so concerned for you. Where are you? What are you doing?"

"Mom, can you come and pick me up?" Lilly said. She was crying. "I'm at a hotel outside of town. Josh just left me by myself."

Peter was out the door in a flash to pick her up. As he drove toward the hotel, he was overwhelmed by questions: *What's happened to my baby girl? Why did she do this? How did she get so full of anger?*

He found the hotel. Lilly stood outside. There were no tears anymore. Without a word, she walked past Peter, got in the car, and slammed the door. The drive home was without conversation. As hard as Peter tried, Lilly would not speak to him. Once they were home, Lilly went up to her room without saying anything. Peter and Janie just shrugged. What could they do? They'd try to talk to her again in the morning.

But at 4:30 a.m., they heard banging downstairs. They both ran down the stairs as fast as they could and found Lilly holding a butcher knife against her wrist. The knife had already drawn blood. "Leave me alone!" she cried. "I'm going to kill myself!"

Peter sprinted to her and struggled to get the knife away from her. Janie phoned 911.

"I hate you, Daddy! I hate you, Daddy!" Lilly screamed over and over. "You don't care about me! You don't love me! You have never loved me! Let go of me!"

WHAT HAVE I DONE?

Relationships are an absolute in life. We cannot survive without them. God created us to thrive in relationship with others, and the results of our relational investments will last beyond our lives on this earth. When the heavy work years of our lives are over, the time we invested in face-to-face personal relationships will matter the most. How much money we made will be irrelevant from an eternal vantage point. How successful a career we had will likely not be remembered as well as the time we spent face to face with those we love. *The fact is that our investment in business relationships will not be remembered as well as the result of our investment in personal relationships.*

It is likely that few people we travel to see for business will remember how much time we invested in them. But our families *will* remember how much time we invested in them—it's part of being a family! The people we have invested the most time in for the sake of business are the people who will care the least when our time of travel is over.

The legacy we leave for the next generation far outlives our physical presence in life. But it is important to remember that *intimate relationships are developed, not purchased.* Providing money for our families will not provide intimacy. No true intimacy comes from money. If we don't fulfill our part in developing relationships with each family member, then someone else will develop them. And this development will survive whether we like it or not. The transactions we make in relationships are absolute. Relationships are eternal.

When we were created, we were inherently wired for relationship. Ever since we were born, our needs, development, and sense of belonging and fulfillment were all directly tied to our personal relationships. We need to think back to our earlier years and ask ourselves who influenced us the most. Was it our fathers, mothers, grandfathers, grandmothers, or perhaps friends? All of us have some very special memories of those people who shaped who we are. Much of our personalities, characters, and mannerisms have come from those influences. Even the bad habits we sometimes pick up can come from these influences in our lives.

How were our lives shaped by these individuals? How did this happen? The answer is simple. It was the face-to-face time we spent with them. It was the daily experience of living in the same house or growing up in the same neighborhood. We are all collections of the time we have spent with special people in our lives.

Here is a fundamental truth: *True, real, fulfilling, long-lasting, and intimate relationships can only be developed face to face. Relationships require our physical presence.*

FAST-FOOD RELATIONSHIPS

What my wife has said to me many times is true. When I am away, "that time doesn't count." For the most part, we put our relationship development on hold every time we go out of town.

Every aspect of our lives depends on the quality of our relationships. Our choices determine what the quality of those relationships will be. Think of it like this: the quality of food is directly related to where we go to obtain it. Choices affect relationships in much the same way: the quality of relationships is directly related to where we go to find them when we crave relationship.

Many times we settle for what I would call fast-food relationships. We leave just when we are about to make progress in their development. Family members see the correlation between time invested at home and time invested away. By our leaving, we communicate that our relationship with them is not that important.

Weeks of travel can leave us burned out mentally and physically. When this happens, we seldom take enough time to enjoy our families when we return home. We're too exhausted, and so our families get neglected. Things that get neglected rust, turn stale, or grow in directions they are not supposed to. Nothing good happens when we neglect relationships. Face-to-face inter-action is the key to developing intimate relationships. With our families, it really comes down to whether we're with them in person.

THAT ITCH WILL BE SCRATCHED SOMEWHERE

When we don't develop the relationships we need with family members, we tend to find relationships elsewhere. In airports, we spend time talking at length to the people sitting next to us before boarding a flight. And we spend time on the airplane speaking to the people seated next to us. Because of the duration of the flight and the captive nature of our face-to-face interaction, some of the conversations may even go a bit deeper. For a few brief moments, we become fast friends with our seat buddies and are able to find some rela-tional fulfillment until our next encounter. Or perhaps we stop at our favorite truck stop, make a connection with the people who recognize us, flirt with the gals who greet us in the parking lot, and engage in interesting and sometimes personal conversations. In these encounters, we think we are encouraged, supported, listened to, responded to, accepted, and acknowledged.

But usually this connection is just a hazy reflection of a true relationship. It's not the deep stuff we crave. But we give this time away to perfect strangers because we are missing our loved ones.

If this sounds ridiculous, we should ask ourselves why it is that we have intimate and deep conversations with complete strangers more often than we do with family members. And if they are good listeners and express care and concern, we might even share very personal things with a person we may never see again. Why? *Because we are wired for relationship.* And if we have not taken the time to develop relationships with the people God has given us to do this with, then we find other outlets. All it takes is a long flight and a stranger who has good listening skills or is perhaps just as lonely as we are, and we will engage in a fast-food relationship. Our need to be known will drive us to engage in deep conversations with someone. And if we're not careful, these conversations might even go too far.

Often a person who would never have a physical relationship with someone outside of marriage will develop a "soul tie." A soul tie is a friend or connection that the marriage partner is unaware of. It can be a face-to-face relationship, an online affair, or just a chance rekindling of an old memory. In reality, it's a fantasy that has already been played out. A soul tie robs a couple of any potential for a deep, intimate connection. The couple is drawn into a three-way or even four-way relationship, where everyone gets less than they need and too much of what they don't deserve.

Look at your secret connections and see if there is a bond to another person. If so, break the bond. Change your e-mail address and your phone numbers, and do whatever it takes to get yourself released from the person who is holding you back from the ones who love you the most.

TIME

So how do we do it? How do we build strong relationships with those we care for most, and so avoid allowing those cheaper versions to take hold of our lives? That's the challenge.

When we come home from long trips, our families have no concept of what we have just been through—multiple time zones, delayed flights, and difficult days on the road create extra baggage for us to carry home. We're tired. We need time to rest and refocus, but our families need time with us. That's the paradox.

What's harder to see is that *we need time with them as well.* A place inside us longs for them. We can fight hard to keep it locked up. We might even tell ourselves that we fulfill our roles by traveling and providing and that is more important than actual face-to-face time. But when that happens, we only end up establishing another fast-food relationship with our families. Family must not be put into the same category as business associates, clients, and strangers on airplanes.

We need intimate relationships, and intimate relationships are only developed through time spent with other people. Intimate relationships require special moments, but those moments can seldom be planned in advance. You might have heard the old adage: It's not quantity time that matters; it's quality time. But really, that's a partial truth. It is quality time that matters, but quality time can only happen when plenty of quantity time is available.

Relationship happens in the morning, when we spend time with our kids wrestling, tickling, or laughing together in bed.

Relationship happens at lunch, when we take our spouses out instead of taking a business associate.

Relationship happens in the afternoon, when we arrive at our child's sporting event, and he sees us in the stands watching and rooting him on. It also happens afterward when we boast about the great play we saw him make or we console him after the play he missed.

Relationship happens in the evenings when we are home, where hundreds of random things happen to cause relationships to develop in special and unexpected ways.

In a life of travel, we push the pause button on our intimate relationships. For example, if we add up all the time we traveled, we might find that ten years of marriage includes as much as three years away from home. We would have had only seven years to develop our relationships. We just lost three whole years of nonrefundable time. Many things can be lost in those three years that can never be regained.

Don't allow that to happen in your relationships. Start making changes now before it's too late.

Questions to Ponder

1. Have you shared personal issues with perfect strangers? In what context does that usually happen? How can you avoid going too deep with people you meet on the road?

2. Who are you developing deep relationships with? Does your spouse know about all of the relationships you have outside of the home?

3. Who is your family developing deep relationships with? Is there anything about those relationships that makes you uncomfortable? What can you do to change that?

6

Short-Term Memory

Memories Need Substance to Be Sustained and Protected

- It's easy to lose sight of all the important memories you miss creating when you travel too much. You can only have those memories if you're around. You can't predict when many memories will be created. You just have to be there to catch them when they come.

- With too much travel, you develop short-term memories, memories without substance that don't last very long. A short-term memory is a memory made without any significant time invested. It's a cell-phone memory, an e-mail memory. It will not last, and it will not fulfill.

- Creating true memories protects relationships. If you cannot remember you are loved, you will not be able to fight off loneliness and temptation.

NOTES FROM SAM'S TRAVELS: IN THE PAST

I am on the East Coast and just about ready to have dinner near my hotel. My son just finished his basketball game on the West Coast, and I think I will call him. Cell phone in hand, I dial the number:

"Hi son, how did the game go? Did you make any baskets?... You did! That's great! What else happened?... You played great defense? That's great too! Dad is so proud of you. Great job. Let me talk to Mom. Hi, honey... I understand Nick had a good game."

"Oh yes," my wife replies, "You should have seen the look on his face when he made that basket. I wish you could have seen it. I will see you in a few days. I love you."

"I love you too," I reply to close the conversation.

I hang up the phone feeling good that I called, but the only real memory I will ever have of this event is a vague picture from a phone conversation. Flatly put, I wasn't there. All I have to reflect on is my son's description of his basketball game.

Memories define our lives, and yet we never stop long enough to count the cost of how much we miss when we travel. Did you ever think that you were *designed* to have certain memories?

If you are a man, you should remember what your wife looked like when she told you she was pregnant with your first child. You should remember being there in the delivery room. If you are a woman, you should remember when your husband proposed to you. You should remember the look in his eyes when you said yes.

You should remember what you did on your first anniversary, your fifth, your tenth, your twenty-fifth. You should have a collection of unforgettable good memories with your spouse.

You should remember your daughter's first loose tooth, her first day of school, her horrible yet wonderful attempts to practice the piano, and the incredible feeling of a million good-morning hugs.

You can only have those memories if you're around. You can't predict when memories will be created; you just have to be there to catch them when they come. For many of us, travel for work is unavoidable. But a big theme of this book is that the amount we travel can only increase if we let it. We mistakenly equate more travel with more success, but more travel only robs us of what we really crave—deep relationships with the ones we love the most.

For those of you who absolutely can't cut down on travel, we'll get to some practical tips for success later on. But for those of you who have a say in the matter, you must take advantage of the opportunities you have to diminish your time away from home.

My friend Nate recently found himself in this quandary. For the past two years, Nate's job has put him on an intensive travel schedule. He has young children, and he vowed that once he was making enough money, he would insist to his supervisor that his level of business travel decrease.

Nate just went to a national convention. The meetings and trade show were in an older building that permitted only very poor cell-phone reception. Nate was distracted by a very full plate of events that day and forgot to head outside to check his messages. The day went by, and after dinner and a night out socializing with co-workers, it was nearly 11:30 p.m. by the time Nate checked his phone.

The first message was from his daughter. "Hi, Daddy, it's Sara. I love you. I am going to my dance recital soon, and I wanted to call you and have you wish me luck."

The second message was from his wife. "Hi, honey. I went to Colin's baseball game today. You should have seen him play. Call me if you get a chance."

The three-hour time difference between the East Coast and the West Coast meant that Nate was still able to call his wife and catch up with her at the end of the day. They felt connected—as connected as they could be. But when Nate hung up his phone, he realized he had missed two events in the lives of his young children. He wasn't at his daughter's dance recital or his son's baseball game. He only heard about them on the phone.

He missed the memory of being there.

Another friend of mine, Len, has been traveling intensely for nearly twenty years. He runs a major division of his company's sales force. He has a lot of responsibility and a great track record of success. He always travels first class, always stays at upscale hotels, and always dines at the finest restaurants around the world.

On one recent trip, Len received a call from his wife. "Len, you are not going to believe it! Charlie [their son] is getting married. He popped the question to Tiffany today. I am so excited!"

"That's great news, honey! Let's celebrate when I get home this weekend."

Later that week when Len got home, they took Charlie and his new fiancée out for dinner. During the dinner, Len's wife pulled out pictures of Charlie's childhood and began to reminisce about the days when their son was young.

"Charlie," said Len's wife, "do you remember that night when you were about twelve and got up and began sleep walking?"

"Yeah, I sure remember that," Charlie said. "I was yelling, 'The sky is falling! The sky is falling!' I have no idea why I did that, but it sure got me to wake up in a hurry."

Everyone laughed.

Another story was told. Another memory. Another laugh.

But Len found that he was laughing as an outsider. He felt as new to the family as his son's fiancée must have felt. His son's life was mostly a blur to him. Most of the memories he had were of the places he was at when he received messages on the road. What dawned on him that night was how much he had missed.

Wow! It sure went by quick, he thought.

ALTERNATE MEMORIES

In addition to incomplete memories, another problem you might experience when you travel too much is remembering things incorrectly. Travelers can actually develop two sets of memories—their own and the separate memory of the spouse who was left behind.

Gina is one such person who was always left behind while her husband traveled for work. When asked about her memories of their relationship, she said, "My memories are of loneliness, isolation, and pain."

She explained, "One time we were at a restaurant with another couple. The woman worked and traveled with my husband. They were reminiscing and laughing about things that had happened on their travels. I felt completely left out. I had no idea what or who they were laughing about. I could have been on another planet for all they knew. My discomfort was building. Then she said, 'Remember the time the hotel was overbooked, and we had to share that room with the boss?' They both laughed and carried on for a while over this. I thought, *Wow. If that had happened to me, I would have told my husband right way—like that same night.* I became immediately suspicious and my intuition was alerted. I had to leave the table and cry in the rest room for a long time. I wished I had called a taxi to go home, but I returned to the table where I remained in silent torture until dinner was over. I became painfully aware that our memories were not the same, not shared, not happy, and I was still very lonely."

Some of the fundamental building blocks of life are the memories of sharing experiences with those closest to us. Memories build our character and prepare us for each new phase of life. It is part of God's design for us and our spouse and our children to develop a deep relationship of intimacy, trust, and love. Our store of good memories is one of the key things we can fall back on when times get tough in relationships and life. When it comes to our relationships, what we know to be true is built on what we remember to be true.

Many of us who travel forget how critical memories are in life. We believe we can check out of our family's life for many years while we make a living and all will still be all right. We rationalize this by saying that while the kids are young we are going to invest in our careers so that when they get older we can spend some time with them.

But the problem is that by the time we are ready to spend time with them, they don't really know us, and we don't really know them. Our kids can honestly say this because they do not have a deep reservoir of memories of times and events with us. Experiencing intimacy requires actually being with someone. Our relationships with our spouses and children will be influenced significantly by the memories we have of experiencing life with them.

THE TROUBLE WITH SHORT-TERM MEMORIES

Instead of building significant memories, we develop short-term memories—memories without substance that don't last very long. These memories are not of strong, personal, interactive experiences. They are of personal relationships that have grown to look too much like business relationships. A short-term memory is a memory made without any significant time invested. It's a cell-phone memory, an e-mail memory. It will not last, and it will not fulfill.

In my twenty-two years of travel, above all, I (Sam) most regret missing the precious years of my three sons' early childhood. I was not a part of those years, not really anyway, and therefore I don't have any strong memories to show for that time.

I (Steve) have many regrets in my life, but there is one powerful area I am grateful for. It is the connection I have with my daughter due to the fact that I fought to get home to be there for her. We have a father-daughter history full of memories we love to go over. We have traveled the world together, and we have stood on hundreds of soccer fields together. My time as a dad has not flown by, because I was there. If you have not been there for your child or children, it is *never* too late to start.

Memories come from the direct experiences we have with others. As we interact with our family members, we observe their personalities, we learn their likes and dislikes, we develop trust and love, we grow in intimacy, and we become fulfilled emotionally. In the end, the memories of the times we experienced together complete the picture of our lives. Our experiences become our memories, and our memories become the building blocks of our souls. And because our memories are defined by our experiences, our lives are defined by our memories.

In a life of constant travel, we are robbed above all of memories. Memories are among the most intimate parts of life. They are things God has designed just for us and our families. There is a special place that God has built into each of us to house these precious memories, but most of the time we don't realize this until it's too late.

Each trip away from our spouses and children is one more set of experiences lost between us. It is one more step in the pursuit of loneliness. A little time apart can be managed, but are we aware how much each of our kids needs us? The compounding effect of each trip we take causes us to risk missing critical experiences at home, and our children will not easily forget our absence.

Take some time to ask yourself some hard questions:

- What do your kids remember about you?
- What do you remember about your kids?
- Who are the specific people you spend most of your life with—what sort of memories do you have of them?

Please hear me well here—I'm not saying to stop making short-term memories. If you're on the road and a phone call is the only chance you get to connect to a loved one, make the call.

It's easy to forget to make phone calls a priority. The excuses are many. We seem to always have a key meeting right at the time of a family member's big event. The time-zone differences create a challenge for us, or we are simply too tired and exhausted from the day of travel to phone home.

But if we commit to taking every possible opportunity to connect, we will schedule into our planners every major event and call right before or after to encourage our children or spouses.

The sad part is that over time, making a phone call can start to feel more like a task than a real interest. It becomes like every other task on our list: something we check off. We want to make sure we accomplish it before retiring for the night. But we mustn't let this happen. Family is too important to be checked off a list.

How easy it is to spend time focusing on a career while the kids are young. But these are the most important years of our families' lives, and we spend those years away from them. Our kids learn to function without us. They learn not to rely on us for anything but money, and they continue to build relationships with others in place of us. After all, that is what we have modeled for them.

Creating true memories will protect and nurture these relationships. Memories provide a foundation—something for our relationships to stand on when times get tough. If we cannot remember how we are loved, we will not be able to fight off loneliness. Eventually we will not be able to fight off temptation.

Take the time to create memories today.

Questions to Ponder

1. How many fuzzy memories do you have of important events in your family's life? Do you often find yourself getting the story of your kids' day over the cell phone? How does that make you feel?

2. Is there anything that your spouse might remember differently than you do because you've been away so often? How do you think your spouse feels about that?

3. How many family functions do not include memories of you? How many memories of birthdays or anniversaries have you missed? How many major events in the lives of your children and spouse include memories of you? What can you do to change all that?

7

Failing in Success

Travel Is an Arena of Great Temptation

- Being away from home too much involves three main dangers:
    1. You're anonymous.
    2. You're often tired and stressed, so your defenses are down.
    3. Your close relationships are severed, so your support system is waning.
- There are three main stages of "failure" while on the road:
    1. You enter into flirtatious relationships.
    2. You look for substitutes to mitigate loneliness.
    3. You succumb to the temptations of addictions.
- Watching for warning signs is not enough. Serious steps must be taken to safeguard your life.

NOTES FROM SAM'S TRAVELS: IN THE PAST

Like a lamb to the slaughter...

Ten o'clock and I'm in my hotel room for the night. I have just fin-ished talking with my wife, and I'm winding down now, watching a little television to help the process.

I jump from station to station looking for something worth relaxing to.

I take a look at the networks. Hmm, what's on tonight? That new sitcom looks good. I'm still playing a game with myself. Deep down, I already know what I really want to watch. I am on a quest. I know I will not watch the sitcom. I flip over and take a look at the movies on pay-per-view. Yes, the current releases, the action, then the drama selection...

Still playing the game.

Okay, why not, let's just see what's on the adult channels.

Looking at the title pages of each one, I stop and read one and then the next. I come to my senses momentarily. This is not want I want to do. I've been down this road before, and it never feels good in the end.

I flip back to regular television. This works for a few minutes, but soon I flip back to the adult channels. Then back to current releases. Back and forth I go, trying to convince myself I am not really interested in porn.

The longer I flip, the more I come back to the alluring darkness of the adult channels. Finally, I cave in, select a movie, and off I slip into another destructive night of pornography.

B eing away from home entices us with a number of factors that, blended together, can create a situation ripe for destruction. When you're away, you're anonymous. No one knows you—you could be *anybody*. You're often tired and stressed; your defenses are down. Your close relationships are severed, at least for a time, so your support system is weak. When you travel, you're on dangerous ground.

I wish the evidence suggested otherwise. But too much time on the road produces a lot of broken lives. Check out these stories.

JOHN'S STORY—A SLOW SLIDE DOWNWARD

John was a successful Christian businessman in his midforties. He considered himself a casual drinker and liked to spend time at the bars in the hotels where he stayed. He would say to himself, *I will have only one drink tonight,* but the truth was that he liked drinking too much to quit after just one. He also liked talking to the people he met in the bar.

John was firmly committed to his wife, but often he would slip into conversation with the women he met in the bars. They were often just as lonely as he was. One scotch and soda after another would lead him through the conversation.

Sometimes he caught himself flirting with these women. When he went back to his room, he was always alone, but he would fantasize sexually about whomever he had just talked with.

The longer he traveled, the more comfortable he became with this routine. One dark night of drinking turned into a darker night of fantasizing. Sometimes he drank too much and passed out in his room. Often he would find a woman's phone number scrawled on a card in his pocket. Sometimes he kept those phone numbers—you know, just in case he needed a "friend" to talk to the next time he came to that city.

The mornings after these nights, John would always convince himself that he didn't have a problem. But another trip would be scheduled, and the pattern would continue.

IAN'S STORY—THE FALLOUT

Another friend, Ian, encountered similar problems. But the frequent traveler in his household was his wife, not him. Here's their story in his words.

I couldn't believe what was happening. She was a singer-songwriter, and travel was typically regular, but not far away. She had many late-night rehearsals and long days in the studio. Her gigs were both in and out of town. When evidence of my wife's unfaithfulness surfaced, I was immediately pulled in two directions. First, I needed to overcome my disbelief enough to confront her with the e-mail from her lover that I stumbled across. How could this be? After all, we had worked so hard early in our relationship to ensure that we were mated for life. Self-help books, endless conversations, and premarital counseling were our "insurance policy." We even found God in the middle of our marriage years. Perhaps it was my imagination or perhaps a mistaken impression. We needed to get this out in the open. After all, we were both married before and had learned from our mistakes. This time it was supposed to be for life. My mind was spinning.

Second, I was overwhelmed with the idea of immediately wanting to fix the situation. I wanted to make it right and find out what we needed to do to repair our marriage. Regardless of how things had been going lately, I knew how good it could be once again. I was not only very much in love with her after many years of marriage, but I felt like I had totally bonded with her. Maybe it was all cloudy thinking on my part.

She was constantly surrounded by guy musicians, but I knew she had God in her heart when she was away from me. And besides, I went to most of her gigs myself. But more and more I knew she enjoyed staying out late. She enjoyed the "artist's" life. I could offer her only the opposite with my white-collar, corporate lifestyle. Over time, real life doesn't seem to hold up well against fantasy. The allure of a different lifestyle, free from responsibilities, free from family approval, free from the burdens of past history, is very attractive.

As soon as that mental break crept in, our life together was on a course to destruction.

There were signs. She seemed to have so many issues with me in recent months. We went to a counselor to discuss them, but her complaints seemed nebulous and without foundation. We had been to counselors before for various reasons, including kid issues, but this time it was different. I couldn't get my arms or my head around the urgency of our problems or exactly what she wanted addressed in our marriage. I seemed to just be a jerk in her eyes at every turn. I didn't compliment her enough. I didn't say the right things. I didn't really like the same things she did. I didn't understand.

I got her a new cell phone as a present; it was the first one she had with text messaging. We both thought it was cool. From time to time over the first couple of weeks, I would play with the phone myself so that I could understand how it worked. One day, a text message came through from her band leader. Then there were more. Sometimes I would come home to find them rehearsing together. He was a great help to her singing career. He also worked at the church where we all went. I knew his wife too. She was a very nice woman. She was the responsible one in their marriage, as I was in mine. Our spouses were the artists who were playful and enjoyable to be around. They were free spirits, and we all went out together on occasion.

My wife and I stopped going to the counselor because it didn't seem to be helping. Over the following months, there were more signs that I was slow to pick up on. I recall the time he left a CD he had burned for her. Not unusual for a musician, but there was also a written message: "Listen to this in private." Along the way, we started to meet with a pastor from the church. Perhaps he could help us. In my wife's eyes, I seemed to not get marriage at all. I couldn't seem to do anything right. She was spending a lot of time away from home now. She was staying with her sister about sixty miles away. I thought it was about me, that she didn't like me anymore. I had no idea that she was weighing our marriage against what she could have in a relationship with her band leader.

One time while she was away, I went out for dinner with a friend of mine. During our conversation he asked me, "Do you think she could be having an affair?" I was shocked and offended at the question. *My wonderful, Christian, faithful wife?* "No, way," was my immediate response. But the question sowed a seed of doubt in my mind.

The text messages, our marriage troubles, the CD message, her continued distancing from me. I was putting the pieces together and becoming suspicious now. She had a three-day business trip out of town planned. She was the guest speaker and singer at a Christian women's retreat. During the week, I had my own management retreat to attend locally. I am in the information technology business and would help her out many times with her e-mail problems. So I knew her password, and I knew she would have limited access to e-mail on her retreat. That's when I found the e-mail expressing her love to him.

When she returned a couple of days later, I confronted her. I thought that she would either lie or "fall on her sword" and ask for forgiveness. Instead, she told me how she wanted to be with him. It was obviously disappointing to her that I wanted to work things out between us. A knife was placed in my heart that day. I could feel my wife and my life slipping away with the wind.

Talks of reconciliation transpired between us. Weak attempts at saving our marriage were made. But it was obvious that she was not in love with me any longer. She and her now divorced band leader were married only three months after our divorce was final. I have been left wondering what went wrong while trying to make that long, lonely climb out of the hurt.

In the years since my divorce, I have gone on many dates. I'm in my fifties now, and the overwhelming majority of the women I meet have been cheated on by spouses or a former boyfriends. Integrity seems to be rare. I hope that people reading this will be willing to sacrifice enough to learn to love their mates forever.

SANDRA'S STORY—A WIFE'S PERSPECTIVE

Sandra's is another tragic story. She tells it in her own words.

We were married in 1979 after living together for four years. We both had full-time jobs and were just getting by. My husband, Ray, changed jobs right after we got married. He was hired by an institutional investment brokerage firm as a research analyst. I was a registered dietician. His area of research was in the computer software industry. He rose to the top fast. He was voted one of the top investment analysts in the country one year. The year we bought our house, his salary doubled. We really thought we were rich then. He was making twice my salary, and eventually his salary made mine look very insignificant.

All of this financial growth came at a huge cost. Ray was on the road all the time. Nearly 75 to 80 percent of our time was spent away from each other. I was alone every Sunday, as he liked to do his traveling on Sunday so he could be ready for Monday-morning meetings. He came home late on Fridays also and was generally too tired to talk or go out. He worked at the office every Saturday to catch up on things he missed during the week. We never saw each other.

When he did come home, he never talked about his work. I never knew where he was or what he was doing. When we went on ski trips with other friends, he took his work with him and isolated himself from the group and me. On two occasions, he even left the vacation early to go on a business trip. I never knew he was leaving until I saw him packing. He did this on many of our personal vacations as well. He also golfed excessively on our vacations, and I was left carrying his golf clubs home from Hawaii or Pennsylvania several times. This was another activity that excluded me, as he played early in the morning alone or with work associates.

I found myself exceptionally lonely. To fill my time, I found sports a good use of my energy. Several friendships came from my sporting activities. As a consolation, Ray bought me a golden retriever puppy to give me affection and keep me company while he was on the road.

Ray was a workaholic and an alcoholic. I became aware of the alcohol problem over time, but once, I was rudely awakened when he came home in his business suit at 7:30 a.m. after being at a business meeting the previous day. I thought he spent the night there. He looked awful and was dirty, and he smelled. As it turned out, he had been locked up all night for drunk driving. He later had to do community service and even go to the white-collar jail for a time. I found out at this time that he had had other arrests in our state and other states as well.

During this time, Ray went through some hard times at his job. He changed companies and did some consulting but was still traveling a lot. He suffered several times from very serious bouts with depression and even tried to commit suicide. He was hospitalized and under psychiatric care. I still knew very little about his travel or what he did.

One day I was looking for some paperwork and discovered his "story," one he wrote for an AA meeting. I was angry, so I read it. That's when I found out he would go to bars to pick up women when he traveled. That was the final straw for me. This was after sixteen years of a very lonely marriage. I felt like a fool. I felt stupid, used, and insignificant. I had never felt worse in my life. I was in therapy at the time for all my sadness and unhappiness. I was not depressed, just lonely and sad. I felt trapped and stuck in a relationship that was unfulfilling.

We were also an infertile couple. I had been through a lot to get pregnant. Most doctors would tell us we needed to have sex more often. Well, corporate travel took care of that, so we finally adopted a baby girl.

I decided to divorce Ray and called a lawyer the day I read the story he'd written for AA. We proceeded to go through the divorce and separation. It was awful. He fought me. He did not want me to leave him but did not love me either. He needed me to stay sane and continue to do all of his caretaking. He could not function well without me. But I knew I had to get out of this sick relationship to save myself and my daughter from his diseases. He became very depressed, traveling all the time.

After a period of time, I met my current husband and began to have a new relationship. Ray did not seem to mind. He even liked Ken. But he still wanted me to live near him and take care of him. He advertised in the paper for dates and found a woman he began to see. His behavior was becoming more and more strange. His travel never let up. So a lot of his weirdness was covered up in the busyness of his work life. But even that was suffering. He got fired. A week or so after he was fired, he told me his girlfriend was pregnant. After ten years of infertility, this information put us both over the edge.

The tragic part is that within a month of this news, Ray was dead. He killed himself in our lake house. I'll spare you those details and the frightening circumstances that led up to them. That is a whole other story.

My husband's travel allowed him to cover up his depression and may have even exacerbated it. The travel kept us as strangers living somewhat parallel lives. The travel allowed him to drink and hang out in bars without any consequence at home. Travel allowed him a secret life. I'll never know what went on in those hotel rooms. I don't really want to know. Did the loneliness he experienced cause him to do things he felt guilty over? Now no one will ever know.

WATCHING FOR WARNING SIGNS

The Bible tells us that there is before every person a very wide and pleasant road that seems so right to follow, but it always, always, always ends in death and destruction (see Proverbs 14:12 and Matthew 7:13). The question is not whether that is true; the question is how much pain you have to endure before you learn it or cross a line and destroy yourself.

Failing in success is very much like falling into success: it just happens. We don't know how or why we let it happen. We can't say we planned for it to happen, but it just does. And we find ourselves one day waking up somewhere far away from home in a very unfulfilling way. We find ourselves alone in another hotel room in another city, and we wonder what went wrong.

While some might think the stories in this chapter seem a bit extreme, the fact is that no matter how many years we have traveled, we can find ourselves somewhere in the cycle of failing. It is a reality of business travel that given enough time away from our families, we will experience a serious personal void. Even though we may think that in our case the outcome of our business travel will be different, we must think again.

We start out as driven men and women and find our success in business comes increasingly with our travel. Then, taking the bait, we increase the frequency of our trips and begin to feel the effects of loneliness. The need to travel and fill the void increases, and travel becomes an addiction. From this addiction comes the tendency toward many other personal addictions that are designed to destroy our personal lives over time.

There are three main stages of "failing in success" while on the road. Initially we enter into flirtatious relationships, thinking we can handle the loneliness. We can see what lies ahead if this behavior goes unchecked or unmanaged, but we still believe we have control over this area of our lives.

Second, we discover we really aren't able to handle the loneliness, so we look for substitutes. Here we are living life right on the edge and flirting with all kinds of temptations. We know what awaits us around the next turn, but now we don't really care to avoid it.

Third, addiction enters our lives. That's when lives and careers that started off so right have become so wrong. In this stage, the addicted traveler lives two lives with two sets of standards. We have one standard when we are at home and another when we are on the road. We now have dual citizenship.

Over time, our spouses and kids will see us more as strangers than as husbands and fathers or wives and mothers. The result, especially with our spouses, is that our families become bitter, distant, and very independent from us. The world does not stop while we are away, and so our families learn to survive without us.

Even though we might have pushed the pause button on our relationships with our families, they cannot push the pause buttons on their relationships with others. Our need for relationship goes on, and so does theirs. They will find ways to survive and flourish without us. In many cases, our spouses will surround themselves with other activities and people so as to greatly reduce their need for us in their lives. They must, for it is a matter of survival.

Beware that in some cases the nontraveling spouse can fall into an adulterous relationship as well. The void can become too much to bear, and our spouses might meet someone else to take our place at home while we're away. Once again, we have failed in our personal lives because we have succeeded in our professional lives.

AT THE PEAK

Watching for warning signs is not enough. Serious steps must be taken to safeguard our lives.

Often we simply end up working harder to keep our two lives more in sync, only to see them grow further apart. Each year we move closer to the edge. The years take their toll, and eventually we will lose our willpower. A deeper drive of loneliness will take over, and in the darkness we fall off the cliff.

This is the cumulative effect of the pursuit of loneliness. No longer are the things we do on the outside able to guard us from failure at work. Why? Because the problem is not on the outside. It is on the inside. Too much travel leads to a level of loneliness that very few people can resist.

And loneliness will eventually be satisfied in any way it pleases. It matters not that we might profess to have the highest moral standards. Whatever we deem to be important in our lives will be ignored and compromised when the cumulative effects of loneliness have their way.

We keep kidding ourselves into believing that we can get close to the edge of relationship failure without ever actually failing. We think years of successful travel without incident means we can and should go years longer. And so we don't see how each additional year on the road damages our relationships with our spouses and kids, as we do not have an active role at home.

We aren't showing love.

We aren't developing long-term memories with our children and spouses.

We aren't embracing the depth of fulfillment in building deep relationships.

We have lost all the nonrefundable moments meant just for us up to this point.

We have become more comfortable having deep conversations with complete strangers than with our spouses.

We have become comfortable calling our sons or daughters to find out what happened at their special events, rather than seeing what happened for ourselves. It doesn't bother us anymore that our spouses can handle things at home independent of us. And our kids have stopped complaining that we are not around, and yet we can't understand why they seem distant or at least unaffected that we have just come home. Our kids develop other lives and are "too busy" to spend time with us, and our spouses are a long way from being ready to really make love to us. And we can't for the life of us understand why all this is happening.

Blindness has become the norm. It seems to us as if everyone is out of perspective except for us. After all, we are the ones making a living and providing financially for the family. We think everything should be just fine between us and them.

This is the result of a radical failure in success. We have been robbed. We are now completely blind, and the effect of attempting to serve two masters has run its course. Money is an evil slave driver, and we have become its slave. *God and family? Why they will have to wait until I get home from one more trip!*

In the very personal parts of our lives, we have found substitutes to fill the cravings of our bodies and souls. These are things we pursue while we are on the road. Loneliness can drive a man or woman to do things in the darkness he or she would never do in the light.

THE PIT IS DEEP

We think that all will be well once we've satisfied that craving, but the problem is that we've begun a downward spiral we cannot easily escape from. Let's take a look at how this might play out with the temptation of pornography.

In the beginning, you only saw a three-minute preview for the adult movies or causally looked at a few adult Web sites. This seemed good enough to fill the void. But now you have to go further and pay to watch a whole movie or become fully absorbed in Internet porn, even if you only watch it for just a few minutes. You convince yourself you will just use this as a means of release after a hard day on the road since you cannot be with your spouse.

Soon you become conditioned, week after week, month after month, year after year, to unrealistic and perverted views of sex in relationships. Sex is simply reduced to physicality without love. It has nothing to do with intimacy, marriage, or commitment. There is no longer conviction inside of you for the consequences for your actions. And you become more and more conditioned to the images you see on the television or Internet. This passing fancy soon becomes an inflamed and full-blown addiction to pornography. You have become a slave.

Then the kind of pornography you watch must be more intense. It must become increasingly filthy for you to be able to respond to it. In the beginning, you might fight the growing urge to watch those adult channels by saying that "this is stupid" or "this is the last time I will watch it" or "a man in my position shouldn't be doing this." So you make a commitment to yourself on your trip home not to look at porn ever again. You have gotten some advice to ask the front desk to block these channels when you check into a hotel, but when you get to the front desk, you feel embarrassed, or you feel it is not necessary, or you think you are so tired that you will go right to bed. So you don't block the channels. In the beginning, you judge your success by how little you have fallen into watching pornography, but over time you find you cannot get through most nights alone on the road without it.

Over time, you no longer fight it. You start thinking this behavior is okay, and you convince yourself that this helps keep you from doing something much worse. In fact, some days on the road are so intense that you actually look forward to abusing your mind and heart with the television. Watching pornography is now on your daily travel schedule. It has entered into your regular mental checklist as something you desire to make time for before you go to sleep.

Soon even pornography will not be enough to satisfy your desires. In your mind you become so conditioned through television or the Internet to sex without your spouse that in the darkness of night, having sex with an actual prostitute seems much better. You find yourself with a new aggression in nightclubs, with attractive co-workers, or even with complete strangers. You develop your addiction to the point of giving in to the temptation of sleeping with someone other then your spouse. You substitute what you have been watching on television with an actual live person. After all, at the height of addiction to pornography, a live prostitute is really not that big a leap to make.

Pornography distorts reality, and pornography controls us. It feeds on loneliness, and like the need for food in times of intense hunger, the need for pornography can come strongly in times of intense loneliness. Willpower cannot resist it, and so, without help, we fall over the edge. But this goes for every addiction we might experience away from home.

The drive to succeed in business, when unchecked and not placed in the right priority in our lives, has no strong counterbalance in which to develop strong intimate relationships with God and family. This type of drive expressed through extensive travel away from family is a recipe for disaster. Most important, this quest for success apart from following godly principles found in the Bible will sooner or later become an expression of both personal and business failure.

The fact is that many of the people at airports live lives full of personal failures, broken relationships, divorces, separations, bitter children, bitter wives, bitter husbands, infidelity, lost and broken hearts, and damaged dreams. Airports are full of very, very lonely people.

We think the worst that can happen to us is business failure. But business failure only creates temporary damage. Personal failure, on the other hand, creates permanent damage, and some would say even eternal damage. As you read this book, how many of you are finding yourselves close to the edge? We strongly encourage you to step back and take a good look in the mirror. How long have you lived close to the edge? One more trip could be one too many. Step back from the edge. Step back now!

I (Steve) liken what some of us are doing to two maggots (just go with me on this) chowing down on a one-week-old dead skunk on the side of the road. It was a fat skunk, so one maggot looks up to the other and says, "Now, this is living!"

That is what *we* do. We consume stuff and work to consume more, and the reality is that all this junk we buy is like skunk meat on the side of the road of life. Wake up! Be a complete human—rounded out spiritually, emotionally, and relationally—and not just a maggot.

Questions to Ponder

1. Are you failing or have you ever failed in your success? What does this look like for you?
2. What substitutes are you currently pursuing in your time away from home? How do these make you feel?
3. What types of things do you seek out in order to help yourself feel better while on the road? What can you do to change this?

8

The Moment of Truth

Where Does It All Get You?

- Too much travel harms you and your family—mentally, spiritually, physically, emotionally, and relationally. The impact can't be ignored.
- If travel manages you, sometimes you will experience a strong, destructive moment of crisis. Hopefully it won't come to that. You can make decisions beforehand that lead to a more balanced life. But if the downward slide is left unchecked, it will lead to a crisis point.
- Even at the bottom, God loves you. There is hope.

NOTES FROM SAM'S TRAVELS: IN THE PAST

It's 10:00 p.m., but I'm not tired enough to go to bed. Alone in my hotel room, I'm thinking about how stiff my neck is from the week of travel and a couple of bad hotel beds. Ah yes, a massage would help. I wonder if I can still get one at this time of night. Noticing a card on my night-stand about the hotel spa and massage services, I call the front desk.

"I'm sorry, sir," the desk clerk replies. "They are closed for the night."

But I have already convinced myself I need a massage. I open the phone book and scan the listings.

I know what awaits me.

With no strength left to fight the temptation, I dial the number.

"What's your room number, honey?" purrs a female voice.

Years of too much traveling had taken their toll. I (Sam) had no safe-guards left. I take full responsibility for the situation I created. I'm the one who decided to lead an imbalanced life for all those years. At the point I made the call to the "massage" service, I was too far gone emotionally to think straight. I had made too many wrong choices for too many years.

I was too lonely to protect myself.

I was too far removed from reality.

I was too much of a proud person to have developed a system of support.

Like an ox headed for the slaughterhouse, I had resigned myself to my chosen fate. I was convinced that I had no way out, and so I fell into darkness and entered a world unimaginable.

The massage service was really a front for prostitution. Years of being driven, years of pursuing success, years of not thinking and only doing, years of pursuing loneliness, years of only creating short-term family memories, years of slowly letting my integrity erode away—this is where I ended up.

Yes, I was a Christian at the time.

And yes, it was a horrible moment in my life.

The morning after, I lay in bed for a few moments, not even knowing where I was. I had been on the road so long that all the hotel rooms were looking the same. I called the front desk to ask the clerk, "What city is this?"

After a snicker, she shot back sarcastically, "You are in Rio de Janeiro, Brazil. *South America, Señor.*"

Slamming down the phone, I sat up on the edge of bed and put my head in my hands. As I remembered the events of the previous night, I felt as though a wave of filth showered over me.

I searched for a way to rationalize it. *It was only one night. No one will ever know. You've actually spent hundreds of nights with "prostitutes" while watching X-rated pay-per-view—this is not that much different.*

Back and forth I went. But I could not explain it away.

Over the years I had convinced myself that pornography was safe, that it provided a harmless way to cope with all the lonely nights away from my wife. But each year I needed increasingly cruder forms of pornography to satisfy my growing loneliness, and this is where pornography had culminated for me.

I was left sitting on my bed with an intense feeling of guilt. Twenty years of unchecked business travel and habits had put me in a place to compromise the one thing I swore to myself I would never compromise: my marriage.

I never felt more alone, more empty, or more distraught than I did at that moment. Lust had always been a part of my life, but this was something different. I had crossed an absolutely forbidden line.

Dropping to the floor, I began to weep bitterly.

How ironic that at the height of my professional success came my most disastrous personal failure.

That night in Brazil was the end of the line for me.

Perhaps, in a way, it was also the beginning.

I had been on the edge of personal disaster for years. Here I was, a much-acclaimed executive, even somewhat of a celebrity in my field. I ran a large organization, always flew first class, and stayed in the finest accommodations worldwide. On the outside, my family was a role model in the community and in our church. My house and cars were all the finest! I was leading a model life.

But on the inside I was torn apart.

The truth is, I hated who I had become. I was overly impatient, demanding, and prideful in most of my key relationships. My selfish ambition had developed to a place that when I looked in the mirror, all I could see was me. No one else mattered. I had two lives, one on the road and one at home. And each year the distance between them grew farther apart. My pursuit of career had become for me a pursuit of loneliness—and a broken heart.

Perhaps your story is similar to mine, or maybe it's not as bad. Perhaps you're quite a way off from doing anything disastrous, or perhaps you've already gone further than I did. Whatever place you're at, you know that too much traveling is doing harm to you and your family. The impact—mentally, spiritually, physically, emotionally, and relationally—can't be ignored. It's a slow, painful death to all the good you're designed to experience in life. Too much travel separates you from those you are designed to be closest to. The big black hole in your life is getting bigger and can't be disregarded any longer.

Unless something changes in your life, you'll get your final wake-up call. The depth of your loneliness will finally overcome you. You will have nothing left: no memories, no relationships, no safeguards. You will have no idea who you are outside of your job. You will exist only for travel, and your personal life will hold nothing but emptiness.

What I have learned is this: if you do nothing to significantly manage travel, it will manage you. And when travel manages you, your only hope of escape may be to experience a strong, destructive moment of crisis. How destructive this experience is will often be up to you. Hopefully, it won't come to that—you can make decisions on this side of the crisis that will lead to a more balanced life. But if the downward slide is left unchecked, it will lead to a crisis point. Perhaps you've already experienced serious, even permanent damage in your life and relationships. Reading these words, though painful, could be a chance to get on the road to recovery.

Fortunately, my story has a very happy ending. After I confessed the details of my night with the prostitute, my wife and I went through a difficult time. During that period, I was able to make some significant changes in my life with the help of some trusted friends.

Today, I am reconciled with my wife and enjoy a closer relationship with her and my children than ever before. I can honestly say I have changed. My wife and I are more intimate than we could have imagined being. My walk with the Lord is back on track.

I still travel, but I travel truly successfully (which for me means *sporadically*), because my mind-set has changed along with my priorities.

The lessons are still raw in my mind—some are still being sorted out today. How did I ever get to the place where I chose to sin by making that call? The answer to that question is why Steve and I have collaborated on this book.

Not every traveler develops a dependency on lust or pornography. For some, it's just never stopping—the business of business. For others, it is gambling or drinking or anything else that comes to own you.

In Isaiah 44:20, the Old Testament prophet speaks of those who are unable to ask, "Is not this thing in my right hand a lie?" So I (Steve) pose this question to you: is what you are doing promising one thing (comfort, relief, euphoria, pleasure) but producing something else (pain, regret, shame, anger, self-hatred)? If so, the road you may need to travel is one that is frequented by many. It is the road to recovery. That road is always open, always an option, and always worth whatever it takes to get on it.

If you remember only one thing from this book, we hope you remember this: any place you travel to out of addiction is really just part of your pursuit of loneliness. May this thought alone motivate you to make some drastic lifestyle changes to protect your heart!

Questions to Ponder

1. How do you think each business trip is affecting your personal life? How does this make you feel?
2. In what situations do you feel you are heading toward a final wake-up call? Who can you talk to about that?
3. Have you experienced a final wake-up call like the one Sam revealed here? (It doesn't have to be the same.) If not, what can you do to avoid getting to that point? If so, where will you go from here?

Afterword to Part II

A Letter from Sam to Any Road Warrior
at the Point of the Final Wake-Up Call

> Therefore, since Christ suffered in his body, arm
> yourselves also with the same attitude, because he
> who has suffered in his body is done with sin. As a
> result, he does not live the rest of his earthly life for
> evil human desires, but rather for the will of God.
>
> 1 PETER 4:1–2

If you have reached the place of a final wake-up call in your life—or if you're not there yet, but you're close—I want to offer a word of hope. Because of the depths I sunk to, I know firsthand what it feels like to hit bottom. It's a horrible place to be.

If you're there today, you may have caused a lot of damage in your life and in others' lives, but it doesn't mean your future is destroyed. God is ready and waiting for you right now. He loves you and cares about you.

Before we go any farther in this book, I want to tell you about the first and most important step I needed to take to begin to change my life.

It was what rescued me from my sins!

The day I hit the wall, everything I loved crashed down around me. I thought I could never be forgiven for what I had done. I knew I would lose everything. I desperately needed help and came back to the place I knew—the cross of Jesus Christ.

Right after my final wake-up call, I fell to my knees and cried out to God for help. He reminded me of the words I knew so well from John 3:16. I felt those words more personally, that God was speaking these words directly to me. God said, *Sam, I so love you that I sent my Son, Jesus Christ, to rescue you. If you believe He can rescue you, He will rescue you, and you will not perish, but you will have life eternally and abundantly.*

As I prayed, I met Jesus. He was right there, even though I had just fallen. I asked Him to forgive me for my sins. I gave Him all my fears of what would happen when I told my wife. I gave Him all my shame of what would happen when my kids found out. I gave Him all my guilt from more than fifteen years of living in this darkness. I repented of my sins, I renounced my addiction, and I asked Christ to take control of my life.

He showed me again how He shed blood and died on the cross to take the place of my sin. The amazing grace and mercy of God rested on me like a blanket of love—indescribable but so real.

The process of forgiveness began immediately. The process of healing began. I trusted Him each day and drew close to Him through reading His Word, praying, and fellowshiping with the close friends in my life.

I saw my fears removed, as my wife and I are now closer then ever before. I saw my shame removed, as my children and I are closer then ever. I saw my guilt removed, as I have been transformed by the renewing of my mind through the daily reading of the Bible and prayer (see Romans 12:2). I can truly say I once was blind and now I can see. Jesus Christ has rescued me and healed me.

In my life I have experienced many things—staying in the finest hotels, exploring the finest vacation destinations around the globe, meeting some of the most powerful people in the world, traveling by private jet, riding in first-class limos, speaking in front of tens of thousands of people, speaking on live-broadcast television and radio. But of all the things I have experienced, nothing comes close to experiencing God's grace! I cannot even begin to describe how amazing God's grace is, but I know His grace is real and it has changed everything inside me.

God's grace gave me the courage to pursue reconnecting with the parts of my personal life that were in great need of repair. As I continued to remember His grace for me, I had the courage to put on the attitude of Christ and allow Him to lead me through a period of discipline, correction, and love that was needed to repair my relationship with my wife.

I encourage you to take a new step of faith today. Renounce once and for all your sin, and let Christ take you all the way through a journey of healing and reconciliation in all your most precious relationships. It is real; He is real, for "if the Son sets you free, you will be free indeed" (John 8:36).

I am forever grateful for all He has done for me.

PART III

The Solution

9

Hope for Your Future

Change Is Possible—Seldom Easy, but Definitely Possible

- One of the greatest decisions you can make in your professional life is the decision to place personal life above business travel.
- If too much travel has become a problem for you, you may not have to give up travel altogether. How much you can successfully travel will depend on how much you need to build or restore the broken areas of your life.
- You can learn to travel without abandoning your family. You can set boundaries and stick to healthy limits. You can also use technology to connect back home and build relationships rather than break them. The key ingredient is your willingness to act.
- To travel successfully, you will need to establish two types of filters—external and internal—and use them in tandem. External filters protect your behavior. Internal filters protect your heart.
- The development of five key personal relationships is crucial to true success. We'll take a more in-depth look at these in the chapters to come. Briefly, they are: (1) God for strength, (2) spouse for intimacy, (3) children for development, (4) friends for accountability, and (5) yourself for balance.

FROM SAM

This statement will sound funny—the antithesis of anything you would ever hear in business school—but it's true: the greatest decision I have ever made in my professional life is the decision to place my personal life above my business travel.

At the publishing of this book, it will be eight years since I made that decision. Today, I am able to travel for work and keep my personal life and relationships intact. If I can do it, so can you.

Every decision I make today related to business travel is based on a fixed schedule of relationship development and time at home. Business travel is managed in light of nonnegotiable times that I have factored in for nurturing the five most important relationships (outlined in the chapters to follow) in my life. I have learned how to make these relationships the number one priority in my life, and the result is that business travel is kept in control.

You don't have to give up travel. Having a job that involves travel may be the Lord's call for you. If so, thank the Lord for His direction in your life, and wholeheartedly pursue His will in your calling. Still, how much you can successfully travel depends on how much work you need to do to build or restore these five critical relationships in your life.

For some of you, the adjustments to your travel schedule will be small. You will be motivated to make these changes for the sake of protecting your relationships from future harm.

For others, the adjustments to your travel schedule will be great. In fact, some of you might need to stop business travel altogether for a season in an effort to restore your most precious relationships.

No matter where you find your personal life and relationships, the following section of the book will help you develop a system that works for you. There is hope ahead.

FROM STEVE

I also learned that you can travel without abandoning your family. You can set boundaries and stick to healthy limits. You can also use technology to connect back home and build relationships rather than break them.

But to do that, you need something no one can give you: willingness! If you become willing—willing to try new things, willing to admit failure, willing to start over—your travel can be integrated into a whole and healthy life.

Hope for your future starts with an acknowledgment that you actually want to pursue hope and take the necessary steps to do so. This statement should come as no surprise, for in anything you are asked to change or improve, you must be thoroughly motivated and committed to make that change.

As business travelers, we will not all be at exactly the same point in our personal lives and relationships. In the context of what you have read so far, we will be in different seasons and phases of our business-travel struggles. But each of us must acknowledge that business travel can be a pursuit of loneliness. Then we must look inside ourselves and acknowledge exactly where we are in the challenges and consequences of travel described in this book.

It is not until we've done the hard work of looking at our situations that the solutions described in the rest of the book will have much impact on protecting our personal lives and relationships as we travel for work. Sam and I pray that if even one thing we've said so far makes sense to you, then in the relevant area of your life, you will ask for help and agree to pursue solutions.

HOPE IS AT HAND

In all my (Sam's) years of business travel, there were two facts I simply did not think much about. Yet later I realized the profound effects these facts had on my personal life and relationship as I traveled for work.

The first is that *all our weaknesses and all our strengths always travel with us.* Our weaknesses grow and our strengths decline if we do nothing significant to protect ourselves when we travel for work. This process is like exercise. The less time we spend exercising, the weaker we become physically. The more time that passes and the longer we live, the more important a significant commitment to physical fitness becomes. We can't just dabble with exercise and make real progress.

The second is that *the most dangerous potential for personal temptation arises any time we travel away from home.* And our greatest source of strength comes from the Holy Spirit as we develop our reliance on Him and our personal relationships.

As we've seen so far in this book, it's easy for our personal relationships to be jeopardized whenever we travel. While our relationships stay at home, our temptations travel with us. When we travel, we leave familiar and personal protection behind. On the road, it's easy to put aside the adequate attention needed to sustain and grow a healthy personal life and relationships. What waits for us is the temptation to find substitutes for success and satisfaction.

So if temptation travels with us on the road while most of our protection stays behind, then we must develop and build strength into our personal lives and relationships in order to effectively counter the deadly negative effects of travel.

Think of it like this: if the things we set up to give us personal strength—such as our spouses, children, family, and friends—all stay at home; if our church and familiar surroundings are all physically left behind when we travel for work, if temptation comes with us and new areas of weakness are encountered on the road, then we must actively work to protect ourselves.

Doing nothing to protect ourselves while we travel is like playing Russian roulette. Sooner or later we will shoot ourselves.

We must proactively develop five key relationships and use them as personal travel filters whenever we are on the road. We'll get to these key relationships shortly, but first, let's address the idea of filters. We'll use this idea throughout the rest of the book.

THE FILTERS YOU NEED

Personal travel filters come in two broad categories—external and internal. These filters must be used in tandem to truly protect your personal life and relationships as you travel for work.

External filters are the things you do on the outside to protect yourself from temptations and dangers while on the road. These filters offer protection from the outside in and help you focus on how to deal with the immediate, in-the-moment temptations that loneliness produces.

Internal filters are the things you do internally to strengthen yourself from the long-term effects of business travel. These filters offer protection from the inside out and focus on how to deal with the long-term development of loneliness and the resulting desire for flirting, substitutes, and addictions.

I learned about the need for filters the hard way. Over the years I tried a variety of external filters without focusing on the internal ones. But I learned you cannot completely control your world with external filters alone. Sooner or later you find yourself in a situation that requires you to dig inside for strength so you can walk away from a compromising situation. External filters will not change you, and they will not change the effects of your schedule on your family. External filters deal with symptoms; internal filters deal with root causes! Only together do they form a complete arsenal of protection.

Let's talk about external filters first.

External Filters

The best tip is to look away (or walk away) from anything that does not belong inside your head or heart. For a full discussion of this method, check out Steve's books *Every Man's Battle* and *Every Woman's Battle*.

In addition, there are some specific things your can do on each business trip. The following list should prove helpful.

- Take pictures of your family with you, and set them out in your hotel room to look at every night. These visual reminders connect you with each person in your family and help you remember your commitment and love for each one.

- Take a devotional book on the road. Read it and journal in it each night. The reading and journaling will connect you to God and help you keep in perspective the bigger picture as you plan for your life.

- Keep a rigorous calling schedule with your family throughout each day and evening.

- Travel with your spouse when and if you can.

- Share a room with a friend, if possible. Always avoid being alone in compromising situations.

- Write to your spouse and kids while in your hotel room at night. Send them letters and cards from the different cities you visit. Keep a close eye on special events and special days in their lives, and make sure you are physically there for as many of those events as possible. And when you can't be there, call at the right moments in the context of those experiences or events.

- Develop an accountability partner (a person of the same gender) or group that you confide in. Give this person or group permission to ask you direct questions about your behavior while on the road. (I will touch on this more in a later chapter.)

- Block the adult channels prior to entering your room by asking the front desk clerk to do it. Ask the front desk to remove the television. Or put a towel over your television and a picture of your spouse on top of the television.

- Stay off the Internet while in the privacy of your room. You can always check your e-mails in a public place such as a local Internet café.

- Schedule your trips in ways to minimize the days you are away. Be sure you map out the cities you are planning to stay in, considering your physical surroundings in those locations. Stay at hotels that have high degrees of safety and security with access to reputable restaurants and fitness centers. Stay in places that have the least likelihood of being near inappropriate bars and entertainment.

- If you are married and you find yourself in a situation where you are alone with another person who is not your spouse, make sure you speak about your spouse often in the conversation. It will help you and the other person maintain the correct emotional distance.

These external filters are great steps you can take to manage a life on the road. As mentioned, however, you cannot manage a life of travel solely from the outside in. The outside-in approach alone shows you how to deal with loneliness by reducing it, eliminating it, or safeguarding your life against it. But that's not enough.

If you are empty in your personal life and relationships, you will not be motivated enough for the external filters to fully work. There is a way around every filter. For instance, you might set up a picture of your wife on your television, but if your relationship with your wife is on the rocks, the picture won't be motivation enough to stay away from porn. Or maybe one month your accountability group is too busy to meet. Or your request for blocking adult channels somehow didn't go through. Combine any failure of an external filter with a stressful day at work or a connection with a perfect stranger, and you are back into a situation of lonely compromise. You cannot address an internal problem with external means alone. External filters alone will fail if not balanced with real nourishment on the inside.

We must develop strong internal filters. These are the missing elements of protection in a life of travel. Moral failures often happen when we least expect them to. For instance, you might meet someone in a café. You strike up a casual conversation. But suddenly that conversation compromises your integrity and the boundaries you've set for yourself.

At that point, a life without internal filters is a house of straw. As soon as a strong wind comes, all the walls of external protection come crashing down. Internal filters address the real pursuit of loneliness. True protection and health can only happen when we start to eliminate loneliness and all the desires that try to capitalize on it. And this happens when we change from the inside out. We must allow the Holy Spirit to transform us from the inside out to truly be protected when we travel.

Internal Filters

Internal filters are what we set up to actively and consciously ensure we are developing three key areas of our lives: long-term memories, purpose, and relationships.

Long-term memories are the opposite of short-term memories or of no memories at all. Long-term memories are what develop when we are present at key events, not just by phone, but in person.

Purpose, as we use the word here, is similar to our identity. We must develop a purpose for our lives beyond traveling and working for income. We have to be known for something other than what we do.

Relationship is the broadest category, because memories and purpose spring from relationships. There are five key personal relationships we must proactively develop. These are the kind of relationships that have been designed just for us. As mentioned, we'll take a look at these in more depth in the chapters to come. Here they are again:

1. God for strength
2. spouse for intimacy
3. children for development

4. friends for accountability

5. yourself for balance

When these five key relationships are developed, we learn how to protect ourselves against loneliness and, by preventing loneliness, eliminate the desire for addictions.

Developing these five relationships begins at home. We can only maintain intimacy with our spouses on the road if what we've developed at home is solid. We can only develop strength from God on the road if we are spending time with God at home. We can only engage with our children effectively while we're away if we are investing in their lives when we're at home. Our friends can only keep us accountable on the road if we are truly accountable to them when we're at home. And we can only develop balance in our personal lives if we have already established a lifestyle of discipline and balance at home in our personal routines.

It is in the face-to-face times that memories are made and experiences are real. And it is at home that we start the process of protecting our lives while on the road. Somehow we are led to believe that we can keep ourselves connected long distance. Yet if we are not already connected, whatever we do on the road will not get us connected! Deep connection with someone requires trust, and the level of trust is directly related to consistency of behavior. If our behavior is not consistent at home, trust for the motivation of our actions while on the road is hard to obtain.

Too often business travelers are told to do extra things while on the road that they do not normally do at home. For example, if you call your spouse while you are on the road, but you do not call much when you are working locally, then a call on the road seems to the spouse more like duty or a substitute rather than a natural extension of who you truly are. The sincerity is missing for your spouse. Regular calls must be a part of each day as an act of love and relationship development.

Relationships take sacrifice, and we must learn to sacrifice time from our careers and other things in order to invest in them. True and trusted friendships are the greatest long-term investments we will ever make. Personal relationships have depth and strength and protect us while we travel for work. They are targeted to develop specific purposes in our lives.

If we want to truly protect our personal lives while we travel for work, we must accept the fact that we can only do so if we sacrifice in the areas that have lasting value to our personal relationships. These relationships will help us develop purpose and fulfillment in our lives. We are replaceable in our work, but we are irreplaceable in our personal relationships. Nothing about them is temporary. They are designed to last. They build on themselves, and the more we invest in them, the greater the return on that investment. How do we stop the pursuit of loneliness? By taking time to make the sacrifices necessary to invest in personal relationships.

You can do this. Take some time to examine your life in light of the questions below. Then give prayerful consideration to the principles of developing the five key relationships as outlined throughout the next chapters.

Questions to Ponder

1. What external filters have you set up to protect yourself? What internal filters do you have to back those up?
2. How well do your filters work? What can you do to enhance them?
3. Think about how you behave toward your family and friends while you are on the road. How different is that behavior from your behavior when you're at home? Why do you think that is? How do you think that affects them? What can you do to change this?

10

God for Strength

Your Faith in Jesus Christ Strengthens You

Quick Tips to Grab on the Go

- How do you maintain strength when you travel? The answer is both simple and complex at the same time: you turn to God.
- You can actually have direct and uninterrupted access to God through a relationship with Jesus Christ. He will give you the strength you need.
- Spend time with Christ and focus on leaning on Him as much as possible. Set up a discipline of reading, journaling, and praying while you are on the road.

GOD, investigate my life; get all the facts firsthand.
I'm an open book to you;
   even from a distance, you know what I'm thinking.
You know when I leave and when I get back;
   I'm never out of your sight.

You know everything I'm going to say
> before I start the first sentence.
I look behind me and you're there,
> then up ahead and you're there, too—
> your reassuring presence, coming and going.
This is too much, too wonderful—
> I can't take it all in!

Is there anyplace I can go to avoid your Spirit?
> to be out of your sight?
If I climb to the sky, you're there!
> If I go underground, you're there!
If I flew on morning's wings
> to the far western horizon,
You'd find me in a minute—
> you're already there waiting!
Then I said to myself, "Oh, he even sees me in the dark!
> At night I'm immersed in the light!"
It's a fact: darkness isn't dark to you;
> night and day, darkness and light, they're all the same
> to you.

PSALM 139:1–12, MSG

How do you maintain strength when you travel? The answer is both simple and complex at the same time: you turn to God.

You see, it is impossible to leave home without *Him*. In years past, whenever I (Sam) traveled, I would always think I was traveling alone and that all my special relationships would stay behind. But that was simply not true.

I came to realize that one relationship always goes with us. One person is never left behind. God is that person, and He is ready at a moment's notice to engage with us, to help us, to encourage us, and to protect us whenever we travel for work.

Our relationship with God is the first personal relationship we must develop. This relationship can be our greatest source of strength. God created us, and He designed us to live forever. He also created a place inside each of us for Himself. God provides the firm foundation for traveling effectively. He is the foundation I have built on to protect my personal life and relationships when I travel for work. Over the years, I have learned to rely on His strength.

There were several questions I needed to answer about God before I could trust Him fully, though. With these questions answered, I know now that God is the only way. They are questions you must come to grips with as well. They include the following.

DOES GOD PLAY HIDE-AND-SEEK?

I remember playing hide-and-seek throughout the neighborhood when I was a kid. Remember the game? You close your eyes and count to twenty while your friends go and hide. Then you go find them.

This is a fun game for kids, but it's not so much fun when it seems like this is how God acts. We sometimes feel that God is hidden in the clouds, uninterested in the details of our travel itinerary and daily lives. We think that He has little to do with our lives on the road. This is simply not true.

Wherever you go, God goes with you. You can't hide from Him. God does not play hide-and-seek. He plays seek-and-find. God promises that if you seek Him with all your heart, you will find Him (see Deuteronomy 4:29, Proverbs 8:17, and Jeremiah 29:13). He is waiting for you to proactively pursue Him as you travel for work.

CAN WE IGNORE GOD?

You can't leave home without God, but you *can* ignore Him. It is amazing that God allows us to do this, but our free will gives us the option. David, the writer of Psalm 139, tells of his experience with God. He says that God is always with us wherever we go. Yet many of us act as if He is not. We have not mentally packed God in our suitcases before we travel. We have not been consciously aware of His presence as our most trusted traveling companion. We have not proactively engaged Him as the one person who can help us the most! Yet God tells us that we cannot hide from Him. He tells us that He is always there for us, even in the darkness of the night when we struggle the most.

God doesn't work in a vacuum. He works through relationships. God will help you 24/7 if you let Him. God never sleeps. He keeps working and watching over you and has your best interest always in His mind.

His plans for you and for me are good (see Jeremiah 29:11). But the questions remain: Are you letting God go with you on your business travel? Does He sit up front with you in the rental car or next to you on the airplane? Is He with you in your hotel room or out to dinner with co-workers? Or is He simply out of sight and out of mind?

The fact is that we can't stop or ignore the development of loneliness and all its temptations without God's help. So why are we ignoring our greatest source of strength? We must engage our greatest source of strength to protect us in the greatest arena of personal temptation and attack on our personal lives and relationships.

DOES GOD KNOW EVERYTHING ABOUT US?

Yes, God knows everything about you. He knows more about you than anyone else does. He cares more about you than anyone else does. And He loves you more than anyone can. There is no place you can go that His presence is not with you. There is no thought you can have that He does not know ahead of time. There is no challenge, problem, or concern that you can have that He is not able to help you with. No one person can help you more in overcoming all the temptations you will face while on the road than God. No one person can give you more help with overcoming the pursuit of loneliness than God. No one knows you better and is more equipped than God to help you. God's caring hand is always extended, waiting for you to grab hold of it.

But the extent of the relationship you have with God depends on you. You can have as much of God or as little of God as you want. God says that He will not force Himself on us, but He will go with us wherever we go, even if we ignore Him (see Revelation 3:20 and Psalm 139:7–10). He allows us to choose how much of Him we want in our lives. The more we have of Him, the better our lives go, because His ways are perfect. God has made it easy to draw near to Him, and He promises that if we do draw near to Him, He will draw near to us.

He will give us the strength we need on the road. Remember: wherever you go, He goes too. It's up to you to draw near to Him.

DO WE GET TO GOD BY DOING GOOD THINGS?

Faith is our avenue to God. You don't have to clear your life up first to come to God. That's like trying to make yourself well before you go to a doctor. You can come to God no matter where you are or what you've done. Just come.

A personal relationship with God starts with a step of faith. What do you have faith in? We all believe in something. And what you believe is ultimately a step of faith.

Faith is how we gain access to God. God says that without faith it is impossible to please Him (see Hebrews 11:6). Therefore, our journey of true faith in God cannot be postponed. It cannot be overlooked, for our lives must be built on foundations of faith. And if we are not growing in faith, we lose our ability to connect to our greatest companion, advisor, and warrior for our good while we travel for work.

The Bible defines faith as being sure of what you hope for and certain of what you do not see (see Hebrews 11:1). No matter how hard life gets while you're on the road, what you believe about God determines what kind of relationship you have with Him. What you believe about God determines how much He can help you. In this complex and amazing world we live in, to think that life just "happened" without a master designer and builder takes much more faith to believe than to believe that God created it all.

It is in a relationship with God the Creator of heaven and earth that we must start to find the path to protect our personal lives and our relationships while we travel for work. But how do we invite God in to be our traveling companion and our closest friend? How do we invite God to be more than just an abstract thought or idea in our lives? How do we know Him as more than just a mysterious thought or idea?

By faith.

DOES GOD WANT TO HAVE A FRIENDSHIP WITH US?

Yes! God has made this clear about Himself in the Bible. The Bible clearly defines the way to gain direct and constant access to God. This way is through believing in Jesus Christ as God and in giving Him your life. In John 3:16, God says that you and I can have a very personal relationship with Him through his Son, Jesus Christ.

The historical records apart from the Bible are clear that Jesus Christ lived at the time in history that the Bible says He did. God came down to earth and took the form of a human in the person of Jesus Christ. The Bible states that "if you confess with your mouth, 'Jesus is Lord,' and believe in your heart that

God raised him from the dead," then we can enter into a personal relationship with Him (Romans 10:9). God says that He loved the world so much that He gave His one and only Son, Jesus, so that whoever believes in Him will live forever with Him!

There is a gap between God and mankind. That gap is called sin. Sin happens anytime we miss the mark of perfection, which is every day (see Romans 3:9–10)! And God bridged that gap by sending His Son, Jesus Christ, into the world to save us. God says the wages of sin is death but that there is a free gift of eternal life through Jesus Christ (see Romans 6:23). This means that a personal relationship with Jesus Christ is a personal relationship with God for today, every day, and even for all eternity.

You can actually have direct and uninterrupted access to God through a relationship with Jesus Christ. Wow! As you read this, where are you? On an airplane? In your hotel room? Are you in a restaurant or taking a break from a business meeting? Wherever you are, you are not alone, and you are dearly loved by God. The truth is that you never have to be alone again. No matter how long or short a time you have spent on the road, Jesus is ready to become your greatest traveling companion.

Jesus is there with you, waiting patiently for you to acknowledge that He is real and available for relationship. He is knocking at the door of your heart, waiting for you to open up so that He can come in (see Revelation 3:20). He is waiting to help you with everything you are dealing with. Jesus says that greater love has no man than to lay down his life for his friends (see John 15:13). We can be His friend if we do what He commands (see John 15:14).

Through His death on the cross, Christ established a relationship with God for us far greater than what many people think is possible. Many think of God as a distant ruler, uninterested in what happens to us. But God's character shows us that He is not distant. When you put your faith in Jesus Christ, He becomes personal and close and calls you His friend.

DOES GOD REQUIRE ANYTHING OF US?

Yes! He is waiting for you to return His friendship.

You may call Him God, but are you ready to call him Friend and take Him everywhere you go? With Jesus as your friend, you have as your ally the foremost authority on protecting and developing your personal life and relationships. Why? Because Jesus was the ultimate business traveler. He experienced the ultimate and most difficult temptations in His life while on the road away from home. No one knows what you're going through more intimately than Jesus. He is inviting you into His world to be His friend.

When you put your faith and trust in Jesus Christ and make Him your primary traveling companion, He becomes your primary friend. The darkness is limited in its power when you are with Jesus. Loneliness is dispelled in the light of your friendship when Jesus is active in your life. The Bible says that if you know Christ, then you automatically know God the Father because God the Father and Jesus are one (see John 10:30). No one is better suited to help you through temptation than Jesus Christ Himself (see Hebrews 4:15).

Some of you believe you are not good enough for God. You have done too many wrong things to be able to get close to God. Nothing could be further from the truth. None of us is good enough to have a relationship with God. We needed Jesus to bridge the gap.

To have Jesus as your friend, you must ask Him to come into your life. You do this when you believe in Jesus Christ as God and receive His gift of forgiveness for every sinful thing you have ever done in your life, including everything you have done while on the road that makes you ashamed. Simply ask Jesus Christ to become the traveling companion of your life. Give Him control of your life. Do this now. If you have never asked Him into your life before, make this moment, right where you are, the moment you experience God's gift of life to you.

Say this simple prayer: *Jesus, come into my life. Forgive me for my sins. Take control of my life. I believe you are God, and I ask you to be my traveling companion forever. Amen.*

You now have the ultimate traveling companion. You will never be alone on the road again.

WILL WE EVER STRUGGLE AGAIN?

Unfortunately, yes. Hebrews 12:1 talks about the "sin that so easily entangles" us. Sometimes God immediately frees us from our old desires. Sometimes it takes a while as He works in our lives and we surrender our lives to Him.

If you are still struggling to speak to God, try to see Him as a friend and not a stranger. If you are not ready to invite Christ into your life, consider how many complete strangers you have spoken to and given parts of your life story to while traveling. How many perfect strangers have you introduced yourself to and sat next to on airplanes or in restaurants or bars? Most of these people you have never seen before and will never see again. Yet you have confided in them on major issues of your life and shared a moment of friendship as a traveling companion.

Instead of sharing all your deepest struggles with a perfect stranger whom you may never see again, why not turn to the Lord today? Jesus knows you better than you know yourself. He cares for you more than any other person can. He is the One who will never leave you or forsake you. He is God's gift to you, and when you do ask Christ to join you as your traveling companion in your life, you enter into a personal relationship with God. God's Spirit lives in you, guides you always, and protects you from the ever-present temptations and loneliness in business travel. The mighty Creator of heaven and earth is your traveling companion as Jesus becomes your best friend. The Spirit of Christ is always with you. As you learn the teachings of Christ, His

Spirit grows in you. The Holy Spirit guides you and strengthens you in all ways.

If you are a Christian already and have asked Christ into your life before, now is a good time to recommit to God as your active traveling companion. As a Christian, you know that it does not matter what you have done or how you have sinned. You can ask Him to forgive you and to cleanse your soul from all that you have been through. Is anything holding you back? Is it embarrassment or fear or shame or doubt? Now is the time to bring it to the foot of the cross and let Jesus take your deepest hurts and secrets and bring you back into God's company, doing God's business.

IS IT POSSIBLE TO DEVELOP A FRIENDSHIP WITH JESUS?

Absolutely! We must learn to spend time with our friend Jesus. We must spend time with Christ with the goal of developing His strength in our lives. The question needs to be asked: do you have time for Jesus? Like all other relationships, it takes time to develop a relationship with Christ. Unlike all other relationships, this one can be developed wherever you are and whenever you go away for work.

For me, this revelation was life changing. I had forgotten how close Christ could be. I had forgotten how much strength comes from developing my relationship with Christ.

The relationship is not without its costs, however. I did not take seriously how much *additional* time I needed to invest in developing my friendship with Christ while I was on the road. I had to increase the time I spent with Him in order to protect all my other relationships while traveling. Once I did that, I realized how much He helped me overcome my weaknesses and temptations while on the road. As the relationship grew, so did my level of freedom.

As we spend time with Christ, His strength grows in our weakness. The more of Jesus we know and the more we follow Him, the less of the bad part of us we know and follow. As we obey God, we grow in His strength. In this relationship, our goal must be to obtain His strength. We cannot depend on ourselves and still survive business travel. We must shift our dependence away from ourselves and onto Christ.

Once I began focusing on learning how to gain my strength through Jesus, my foundation became much stronger. And as my strength grew, my ability to travel with my relationships intact improved. As my ability to maintain my relationships during travel improved, I could travel for work with far greater strength and with far greater protection in place.

On every trip we enter a danger zone full of traps for our personal lives and relationships. We have tried to depend on ourselves for too long, and some of us have not had the strength to make it through unscathed. We easily run out of gas when we depend on ourselves. Therefore it is important that we learn to depend on Christ. He was tempted in every way, yet He did not sin (see Hebrews 4:15). He is the only One who can truly give us the strength we need while we travel for work. But how do we learn to depend on Christ?

First, we must make a commitment to invest in this relationship through prayer throughout the day.

Second, we must establish that our primary goal is gaining strength through His Word. We experience His strength by learning what He taught us and by following His instructions. We must spend time in His instruction manual so that we can know how life is supposed to operate. Christ reveals more of Himself every time we read His Word. Our relationship with God can only grow if we spend time with Him.

Finally, we must connect with other believers. We can't do this alone. Find a good church that teaches directly from Scripture. Commit to regular attendance for you and your family. Develop a trusted group of friends and journey together spiritually.

WILL CHRIST FIGHT FOR US?

One of my favorite portions of Scripture describes a battle:

> The world is unprincipled. It's dog-eat-dog out there! The world
> doesn't fight fair. But we don't live or fight our battles that way—
> never have and never will. The tools of our trade aren't for market-
> ing or manipulation, but they are for demolishing that entire
> massively corrupt culture. We use our powerful God-tools for
> smashing warped philosophies, tearing down barriers erected
> against the truth of God, fitting every loose thought and emotion
> and impulse into the structure of life shaped by Christ. (2 Corinthi-
> ans 10:3–5, MSG)

How often have you felt you were in a battle to protect your personal life
and all your key relationships? It's easy to try to fight your battles yourself
when you're on the road.

But of all the battles, the ones inside us are the most difficult. We are constantly bombarded by disastrous thoughts. These are thoughts that, if acted
upon, would destroy us and the people we love. It is here that Christ comes to
help us the most. We must learn to take every thought that enters our mind
and give it to Christ in prayer. We must memorize Scripture and quote it when
we need His strength. He is the One who offers to fight our battles, and He
never loses a fight!

WHERE CAN WE FIND STRENGTH?

It sounds paradoxical, but it's true. When we are weak, we are strong. Our
strength comes from relying on the Lord. Consider this scripture:

And then he told me,

> My grace is enough; it's all you need.
>
> My strength comes into its own in your weakness.
>
> Once I heard that, I was glad to let it happen. I quit focusing on the handicap and began appreciating the gift. It was a case of Christ's strength moving in on my weakness. Now I take limitations in stride, and with good cheer, these limitations that cut me down to size—abuse, accidents, opposition, bad breaks. I just let Christ take over! And so the weaker I get, the stronger I become. (2 Corinthians 12:9–10, MSG)

If ever a time comes when you think you can't go on another day, remember those words. The New International Version puts it this way: "My grace is sufficient for you, for my power is made perfect in weakness" (2 Corinthians 12:9).

Depression can come when we feel defeated or have lost too many battles, but it is at this point that Christ does His best work! When we feel we have no power or ability to protect ourselves, He is willing and able to take charge. As you learn from Christ and obey what He says to do, you will be able to hold on tight to your faith in Him. The result is that He will guide you out of the darkest places and keep you safe as you travel for work.

Spend time with Christ and focus on leaning on Him as much as possible. Let Him fight your battles. Find His strength when you are weakest. Set up a discipline of reading, journaling, and praying while you are on the road. The best times are often in the morning when you first wake up. Ask Him to protect you during the day. Another good time is in the evening. Ask Him to protect you during the night when you are most vulnerable.

There are many tools available at Christian bookstores and churches. These include devotional study guides, *The One Year Bible,* and daily reading plans and journals. The bottom line is that you must spend more time with Jesus while on the road than you do at home. Whatever you do at home must increase while you are on the road. The end result is that you have added a layer of protection in your life against developing a pursuit of loneliness. God is your strength to stop the pursuit of loneliness!

My wife and I (Steve) created a great tool for you. Actually, there are two versions: one for men and one for women. It is the One Year New Testament for Busy People. Spending five minutes a day in it will take you through the New Testament in one year. We provide some things to think about in each daily section. Five minutes is a great place to start in growing closer to God. You will be amazed by what five minutes can do to enrich your Christian life.

Questions to Ponder

1. Do you have a personal relationship with God? What does that look like in your daily activities?
2. How much time each day do you spend with God? What can you do to increase that time?
3. How does your relationship with God change, if at all, while you're on the road? Does it feel stronger or weaker? Are there any ways you can change your approach to that relationship while on the road?

11

Spouse for Intimacy

Your Spouse Is Your Greatest
Return on Investment

- After God, the greatest relational investment you can make is in your spouse.
- There are six key external activities that will help you build strong, long-term memories with your spouse and allow you to sustain intimacy with him or her while you are on the road. These activities include:
    1. laughing together
    2. encouraging each other
    3. touching each other
    4. talking about your feelings
    5. forgiving and being forgiven
    6. protecting your image of your spouse

Kiss me and kiss me again,

> for your love is sweeter than wine.

How fragrant your cologne;

> your name is like its spreading

> fragrance.

SONG OF SOLOMON 1:2–3, NLT

How do you protect intimacy with your spouse when you travel? You have to invest in it.

After God, the greatest relational investment you can make is in your spouse. There is no other person on this earth that God has designed to care for you more. Next to your relationship with the Lord, this is the second-most important personal relationship that you must develop. True intimacy is part of God's design for you, and the intimacy of marriage affects every part of your life—emotional, mental, physical, and spiritual.

At the beginning of time, God created a man and a woman to be together to glorify Him and to express His image on earth. When we recognize that this is our primary goal in a marriage relationship, we understand that marriage is the best place to find true intimacy. In this union He said that the man and the woman were to become *one flesh* (see Genesis 2:24). A man and woman joined in marriage are designed by God to become more than just friends and family. They actually become *one*.

This intimacy God is describing includes sex, but it is so much more than that. It is a union of heart, mind, and soul that takes place in the spiritual realm as well as the physical. Scripture compares this union's uniqueness to the love that Christ has for His people. Those who have chosen to follow Christ have access to God in an intimate way that supersedes any relationship on earth. The union of a man and a woman in a God-blessed marriage mirrors this union between Christ and the church.

The primary goal of marriage is for a man and a woman to experience the intimacy God has designed. It is the highest calling in a personal relationship. Likewise, the greatest physical experiences can only come within this relationship. The ultimate satisfaction of all the senses has been designed for this union. As you open your eyes and realize that God created a spouse for you, you realize this is who God uses to complete and fulfill you.

The world bombards us with the idea that intimacy means sex alone and can be found anywhere. The majority of all programs on television show love and sex outside of marriage as if this were the desirable norm. We are inundated with sights and sounds of people attempting to lure us away from experiencing true intimacy with our spouses. The media portray sex as special and enjoyable only outside of marriage. This is all a lie. The further we drift from developing intimacy with our spouses, the further we get from one of the greatest blessings and experiences God has created and designed for us.

No two people will experience intimacy the same way. God has designed this most special gift of intimacy for us to experience uniquely with our spouse. Can you imagine that God has designed a person for you to fill a place of intimacy that no one else on this earth can fill in quite the same way? Such a union is an indescribable mystery. No two unions have ever been alike in the thousands of years of human history.

The ultimate goal of intimacy is to give us a glimpse of what we will experience in heaven through Christ. As we become one flesh with our spouse, we find a picture of how, someday in heaven, we will be one with Christ. God's design for intimacy is that it be the foundation for long-term trust, attraction, desire, connection, and friendship. Believe me when I tell you this—these things can only be experienced to their fullest within a marriage relationship! Nothing on the road even comes close.

When God created the heavens and the earth and then completed His creation with man and woman, the last thing He said about it all was that it was "very good" (see Genesis 1:27–31). This is another way to say that it was perfect in design and potential. Consider: if God created marriage and said that it was very good, then could there be anything better? Knowing this relationship has so much potential is the beginning of knowing how valuable your investment in your spouse will be.

Impossible, you might say. Perhaps you have slipped into such a rut in your marriage that there is very little left to invest in. You might think that God is disconnected from you and you from Him. But there is good news. Even if you have fallen away from God, nothing is impossible with Him. All it takes is a willingness to be honest with Him and humility to admit you need help. He can and will help you restore what you have lost, but it requires a real commitment to invest. Relationships take time and sacrifice, but your relationship with God and your relationship with your spouse are worth all the effort in the world.

FOUNDATIONS OF INTIMACY

With intimacy as the goal, God gives us a set of radical instructions to get to the heart of how to develop intimacy between a husband and a wife.

To the husband God says: love your wife enough so that she knows you would be willing to die for her! She'll know this because of the way you treat her on a daily basis. Learn what your wife loves and how to love her. If you struggle with this, Christ says to just do what He did. The apostle Paul wrote, "Husbands, love your wives, just as Christ loved the church and gave himself up for her to make her holy, cleansing her by the washing with water through the word" (Ephesians 5:25–26). Imitate His example of sacrifice.

God also says it is the husband's responsibility to take the lead in learning the truth of God's Word. Everything you need to know to do the will of God is found in the Bible. As Christ loves the husband, so the husband must love the wife. How do you know when you have arrived in love? Christ's answer seems crazy—He says to be willing to die for her! When your love is so deep that you are willing to die for your wife, then she will be one loved woman! The level of intimacy will be so fulfilling you will have no desire to pursue another form of it elsewhere. Doesn't that sound good?

And to the wife God says: love your husband in a way that honors him (see Ephesians 5:22–23). He needs to know that he plays an important role in your life and that you value his contribution—even if you are the major breadwinner.

Christ says your calling is to understand and support your husband (see Ephesians 5:22). One of the foremost desires a woman has is for her husband to demonstrate true intimacy beyond the realm of sex. This seems to be one of the biggest disconnects in marriages, especially marriages under the demands of travel. Men seem to cover up their desire for true intimacy with their desire for sex and are quite often misunderstood as a result. But God gives a wife a clear way of communicating with her husband's desire for true intimacy: submission. Now, before you bristle too much at that suggestion, know that the word used for *submit* in the original Greek text essentially means "to show respect."

In the case of a woman who travels for work, her husband will need to know that she is devoted to respecting him more than her boss or business partner or customer. Regardless of her status at work, he needs to know that she's his biggest fan. Something amazing will happen when a wife seeks to understand and support her husband. A woman is not supposed to be anything less than she was created to be. She is called to invest in supporting her husband as God designed. This is the realm where true and deep intimacy is developed. Every hope and dream a woman has for her relationship with her husband will be realized as she follows God's plan for investing in intimacy. The more a wife respects and supports her husband, the more her husband will seek her as his greatest source of intimacy.

In both of these approaches to intimacy, the development of love is far deeper than anything a man or a woman can experience in any other way. The type of love God has created to be experienced in marriage was defined by Christ. God wants us to experience this type of intimacy so we can understand how much He loves us.

Now let's look at the best ways to develop this type of intimacy within our marriages.

HOW TO DEVELOP INTIMACY

There are six external activities that can help you build a strong intimacy in your marriage that can be sustained while you are on the road.

1. Laughing Together

Laughter is a doorway to intimacy. It is like an instant vacation in a marriage and the best way to keep perspective when things go wrong.

If you laugh together, you can cry together, and thereby feel more ready to trust each other when communicating feelings. If you can find humor in everything, you can survive anything. Do not take things so seriously. Learn to stop yourself when you are ready to get angry and instead use the love language of laughter. If this is your behavior at home, then you can take this behavior on the road through phone calls and little creative things you can do while you are away.

2. Encouraging Each Other

Become each other's cheerleader. Learn how to encourage and support your spouse's activities. Listen and really take an interest in the things your spouse likes to do. Express respect for your husband. Every chance you get, compliment him in public and in private. Build up your wife in front of others and give her honest credit for your family's successes. Let your spouse truly know you appreciate him or her. The more we build up our spouses, the more they will feel valued by us and build us up in turn.

3. Touching Each Other

The power of intimate touch cannot be underestimated. You must develop a healthy habit of touching each other beyond just the bedroom. Intimate touch is the love connection of holding hands, cuddling, stroking each other's hair or arm or leg, and other ways of showing physical affection. Too frequently I run into couples who do not touch each other, especially in public. Remember when you first got married, how often you were in each other's arms? Bring those days back!

Touch is the basis on which couples develop a healthy desire for each other. Touching your spouse protects you from wanting to touch others in a world of many lonely people. Touch protects you from finding a substitute for what God has designed for your marriage. If a husband and wife do not touch each other, a secret desire for affection will begin rearing its head while they are away from each other, be it for business or any other reason.

Intimate touch does not have to include sexual touch, but we must develop a language of sexual touch with our spouse as well. Be honest and open and explore together. It is the most wonderful exploration you will find, and it is exactly what God wants you to do! If you learn to touch your spouse, you will lose your desire to touch someone else. Only your spouse can fill that void for sexual intimacy inside of you.

4. Talking About Your Feelings

One of the biggest barriers to growth in marriage is the absence of discussion. Couples must talk about their feelings. Life is not perfect, and marriage is not perfect. Your spouse is not perfect and neither are you. Your call is to talk to your spouse about how you feel and what you struggle with.

Traveling with unresolved issues can actually cause a heart to grow colder.

Studies generally agree that the average woman speaks twice as many words per day as the average man. The question is: are they talking to each other? For women this comes easier, but it is just as important for men. This means that we must make sure we are speaking to each other every day about more than just the kids, work, and the home. We must work at speaking about how we feel—our anger, guilt, fears, hopes, and dreams.

Set aside time each week for just the two of you to go out and talk. Tell your spouse what happened each day and what challenges you had personally. If you learn to invest time together while you're at home, your time on the phone will increase in meaning and depth while you're on the road. Call your spouse as frequently as you can while on the road—at least once a day.

5. Forgiving and Being Forgiven

We must not let resentments build up in our marriages; we must learn to forgive our spouses and ourselves. Conflicts in marriage happen, and we need to give our spouses permission to tell us what they are struggling with. Everyone's feelings are valid. We must get to know how our spouses feel on issues that cause conflict between us.

If we do not, those feelings will fester and grow cold. Not sharing with each other is the biggest way to cause a separation in a marriage. If you do not share and forgive, you are not in a place to see your spouse or yourself properly. We cannot express love and receive love properly if we do not forgive.

What hurts do you need to forgive your spouse for? What do you need to ask your spouse to forgive you for? We will only be forgiven to the extent we forgive others. This is the best way to ensure freedom in communication with your spouse while you travel for work. If there is an issue that needs forgiveness, then work that through before you go out of town. This may be the hardest thing you will have to do if you have suffered from addictions while on the road. But I know from personal experience that it will be the best thing you could ever do. There can be great healing through forgiveness.

6. Protecting Your Image of Your Spouse

This is the biggest vulnerability to attack you will face when on the road. Intimacy with your spouse must not only be developed, it must be protected! Our images must be real, not make-believe. What we see on pay-per-view or over the Internet or in the seat next to us on airplanes or restaurants is not a *real* source of intimacy. If we look at other images as sources of physical intimacy, we set ourselves back and block our view of seeing things clearly. If we think about them and meditate on them, we rob ourselves of true intimacy. To develop trust, we must develop intimacy with our spouses. We must set our minds on our spouses and not allow the constant barrage of false images to enter in.

When you begin to find true intimacy with your spouse, you will lose your desire for substitutes and instead try to protect your relationship. The goal must be to seek and search for those things in your spouse that will grow your love and intimacy. Your spouse must see this in your actions as well as your words. Your spouse must be the most important person in your life. You will receive back only as much relationship, intimacy, and life as you first give to your spouse.

Questions to Ponder

1. In which of the six areas above do you need to invest more with your spouse? Where would you like your spouse to invest more with you? Set a time to sit down and talk about this with him or her (tip: talk about the ways in which you would like to change first!).

2. What changes do you need to make at home to support your relationship with your spouse on the road?

3. What do you need to forgive your spouse for? Where do you need to ask for forgiveness? What changes will you make after you do so?

12

Children for Development

Your Children Develop You

Quick Tips to Grab on the Go

- One way of investing in your character when you travel is to proactively develop the character of others. When you commit to building into the lives of your children, it can motivate you away from loneliness and toward health and balance.
- Five principles will protect you and your relationship with your children:
    1. Remember that they are always watching.
    2. Be their teacher.
    3. Engage them on their terms.
    4. Make the weekends a nonnegotiable time with your family.
    5. Look into their eyes.

What is another way to protect your character as you travel? You can invest in developing the character of others. One key to protecting your personal life is to invest in the training of your kids. Proactively teach your kids how to behave and how to treat others. Teach them right from wrong and how to develop their character. When you have a solid commitment to seeing your children succeed, this can motivate you away from loneliness and toward health and balance.

The following two examples are stark reminders of how our lives affect our children. Unfortunately, one story is an example of how we should interact with our kids, while the other is not. Take a look to see if either of these stories represents the current state of your relationship with your children:

Katie's Drawing

Katie was eight years old. One day when she was at school, her teacher said, "Now class, I want you to draw a picture of what you and your daddy like to do together."

Katie, after thinking, picked up her crayons and started drawing. After a little while, the teacher said, "Okay, let's share our drawings with the others."

When it came to Katie's turn, she held up her picture and said, "This is an airplane, and my daddy likes to fly on airplanes, and we say good-bye to each other a lot." When the teacher looked at the picture, she saw an airplane with little Katie alone, waving, and the words, "Good-bye, Daddy!"

A Letter from Louis

Dad, you're the best! I love you and thank God for you and Mom all the time. Thank you for the great birthday present and for the wonderful party. Now that I am twenty-one, I pray God blesses me with the strength to follow Him in light of new temptations. I also pray that I can become a man like you, Dad. I respect and seek the love you have for God and hope to one day love the Lord as you do. Who knows, maybe one day we will run a church together. I love you, Dad!

When we travel too much, our children too often view us the way little Katie saw her dad. Our kids love us, but we're always saying good-bye. The second note shows how obstacles can be overcome. It's an actual note from my (Sam's) son Louis. I have three boys, and though I've made mistakes along the way, all three of them have benefited from my commitment to invest directly in their development.

I did not always give my boys the time they needed. As my travel increased, my time with them decreased. When I started to see the negative effects of spending less time with them, it was the one thing I worked hard at improving. As I invested more time in them, I saw a tremendous improvement in my relationships with each of my three sons. Time and attention made all the difference.

If you have children, commit now to actively participating in their development. As they grow, you grow. If you are single or do not have children, then actively invest in mentoring someone younger than you.

Proverbs indicates that children primarily learn from watching their parents. Think about your childhood. You learned from your parents, either by what they did to train you, or by what they did not do. Either way, you learned much from them. This is how character is developed. Some parents say, "Do as I say, not as I do." This simply does not work. Long-term behavior is modeled by parents, either positively or negatively. God gives each of us the responsibility to train our children in the way they should go.

The principle of modeling is key. God says that if our children receive good modeling, they will know what to do when they get older. Yet this is the one area we tend to pay the least attention to as our business travel requirements and demands increase. But it is the most important assignment we are given by God. It is one of the ways He blesses us and grows us and protects us. We are designed to be the ones our children look to to find their character. And whether we train them or not, they will learn from us. As we consciously and carefully model life for our children, we can give them the tools to protect their lives and build their character as they get older.

FIVE PRINCIPLES FOR INVESTING IN OUR KIDS

As we teach godly character, we are motivated to live with godly character. God uses this principle to speak into each of us as we invest time teaching our children. To teach someone else, we must learn exactly what it is we are teaching. The best way for us to build our character and protect our character while on the road is to invest time in developing the character of our children.

Five principles will protect you and your relationship with your children.

1. Remember That They Are Always Watching

Whenever we have someone watching us and looking at our behavior, we set up a strong protective shield of responsibility in our lives.

As we travel, we must take extra care to proactively invest in mentoring others. Think about all the times you spend being on your best behavior. When we go to a client's office, to church, or to a function, we tend to keep tabs on what we say and do. There is a built-in motivation in each of us to be our best in front of others.

God can use this motivation to protect your character. Every time you are tempted to compromise, you must remember that your children are counting on you to teach them the right way to live. As you commit to teach them character, you stay mentally engaged in how you model character. Every day you are away, this will be at the top of your mind.

2. Be Their Teacher

How do you get something to grow? You focus on its health. Healthy things grow automatically.

Whenever you focus on teaching your children healthy things to do and be in life, they will grow in healthy ways. The best way to help them grow is to be their official teacher. As their teacher, prepare your lesson plans while traveling. This becomes a forced discipline that keeps you engaged in their development even when you are not with them!

I am not advocating elaborate lesson plans or a training curriculum. Simply taking time to find one thing in the Bible to teach them each week would be great. It's not hard. Just take a few moments in your hotel room to study. Bring a study Bible with you and read and write a few things that you would like to teach your children when you get home.

You could start in the book of Proverbs and teach them wisdom, or start in the gospel of John and teach them about Christ. You do not have to be a Bible expert. Just read, tell your kids about what you read, ask them open-ended questions, and listen.

You may want to set a day and time each week to go over what you've learned with them. Make it a fun time; for example, you might take your son or daughter out for ice cream and study the Bible together. Or you may want to informally teach your child as subjects naturally arise in conversation. Some of the best teaching times happen while driving kids to baseball practice or home from school.

3. Engage Them on Their Terms

What is your son or daughter interested in? Soccer? Dance? Video games? Math? Learn your children's interests and spend time with them on their terms.

You must be there for their special events. As much as possible, schedule your business travel around the key events in their lives. The best lessons come to them when they learn that you are sincerely interested in their lives. And these lessons come only if you are there when they go through the different stages of life. Phone calls, explanations, and excuses are not the same.

Of all the appointments you make, the ones you make (and keep) with your children will have the highest lasting value! They are learning from you and will learn the most when they see how much you care. Every day is full of nonrefundable moments with your kids. Work hard to be at critical events, and talk to them each night you are away at noncritical times. Engage them while you're at home, and they will engage you while you are on the road. Your phone conversations will be more productive, and you will find fulfillment that will sustain you as you travel for work.

4. Make the Weekends a Nonnegotiable Time with Your Family

As much as it depends upon you, make it a priority to be at home on the weekends. Establish this boundary with your employer. Weekends are for family.

Your kids will look forward to the time you spend with them on the weekends. Don't be too tired. Don't be preoccupied. Don't schedule other things on the weekends. Schedule your kids in! If it becomes necessary to be at a critical meeting on a Monday morning, take a red-eye flight! Do not compromise this time with your children.

5. Look into Their Eyes

Pay attention to your children. Give them your full focus. Don't ever take time with them for granted. Invest in them actively, faithfully, and diligently. You will never regret spending time with your children.

It's easy to be preoccupied, even at home, with phone calls, e-mails that need answering, and extra work that needs attention. But make home time *home* time. Set it apart. Your children should understand that sometimes Dad or Mom needs to make an important call from home and might need some privacy, but for the most part, home is not a place for work. Home is a place to focus on family.

YOUR CHOICE TODAY

Having a solid commitment to seeing your children succeed can motivate you away from loneliness and toward health and balance. It's seldom easy being a parent, but no one is asking you to be perfect. All that's required is willingness.

The most effective parenting tool for me (Steve) is the admission that I may not always know what I'm doing. For instance, when my daughter Madeline reached thirteen, I told her I didn't know how to be a dad to such a beautiful teenage daughter. (She thought that was my job). Yet I told her I would do my best and learn. You are never stronger than when you admit to your kids that you—like them—have a weakness or two. Besides, they know that already.

Your kids need you. And strangely enough, you need your kids. You need them in your life in order to be the person of God you need to be.

Questions to Ponder

1. How much time do you spend with each of your kids each week? How about as a family? What can you do to increase that time?

2. How do your kids feel about your travel? What can you do while you're at home to help them feel better about your times away?

3. What have you taught your kids by your actions? Is this different from what you've tried to teach them with your words? How can you reconcile those differences?

13

Friends for Accountability

Your Friends Watch over You

Quick Tips to Grab on the Go

- It takes one or two trusted friends to "do life" successfully. The time you spend with trusted friends is an incredible investment.
- Close friends help keep you accountable. Accountability means you maintain a strong connection to the people in your life who know the real you.
- Accountability has three main components: support, visibility, and a plan. *Support* is all about staying in touch. *Visibility* is all about direct questioning—give your friends permission to ask you hard questions about anything. Once something is discussed and brought into the light, it loses its power to control you. A *plan* puts you on the offensive to ensure you stay away from troubles and struggles before they occur.

W hy do we ever think we can "do life" alone? It takes one or two trusted friends at least to make the journey successfully. The time you spend with friends is an incredible investment. I (Sam) know this firsthand.

It was three days before Christmas several years ago, and my family and I were making final preparations to drive several hours down to my parents' house for the holiday. A reunion was planned, with my siblings and their families coming in from all over the country. This year was especially exciting because our extended family had not all been together for a while. Two days before I was to pack up the SUV and drive south, I received a phone call that would forever change my life.

"Sam, this is your brother-in-law Larry."

"Hey, Larry, what's up? We are right in the middle of dinner."

"Sam, I'm so sorry… Your father just passed away."

I was in shock. After a long pause, I asked Larry what had happened.

"Well, we don't know for sure. We were told it was a massive heart attack. His body is still at the hospital."

"Larry, I am on the next plane. I will be there as soon as I can! Who have you been able to get ahold of?"

"Your sister Gina [Larry's wife] is with Mom right now. They are both in really bad shape. I can't get ahold of Angela. Your sister Mary is en route on a plane as we speak. I don't think they're scheduled to land for another four hours."

I hung up the phone. A three-minute phone call had suddenly shifted my life and immediate priorities very drastically. I didn't know what to do. I walked around my house several times, feeling completely helpless. Hundreds of thoughts and emotions flooded my mind. An overwhelming sense of responsibility came over me. I could not cry, at least not as much as I needed to. I knew there were too many immediate things that would need to be done. I was the oldest and would be expected to take charge.

My parents had not planned for this. My dad was only sixty-two years old. As I threw a bunch of clothes into a suitcase, I knew there would be very difficult days ahead. I felt desperate to find a solution to help comfort my mom until my other sisters and I could arrive.

And then I thought, *Wayne!* He lived only twenty-five miles away. As I ran out the door, I simply said to my wife, "Call Wayne."

I met my good friend Wayne when we were both only five years old. We grew up together in one of the many suburbs of Los Angeles. Both of us lived in very small homes surrounded by busy streets, open fields, factories, train tracks, and oil refineries. It was a humble life but a virtual paradise for two small boys with bicycles, backpacks, and lots of imagination. We explored, played, dreamed, stumbled, fell, got hurt, got into trouble, and bailed each other out. We experienced our first of everything together as we grew up. Whenever we get together now, we are still very much kids at heart. When the chips are down, we know we can count on each other.

When I arrived at the hospital to begin to make the arrangements for Dad, I looked up and there was my friend. Wayne had already been there for several hours. He had dropped everything to help. He came with no questions asked and no direction given. He just came. This meant more to me than anything any friend could ever do.

WHEN NO ONE KNOWS YOU BETTER

There are few things in life as precious and fulfilling as our friends—the people who guide us, hold us, encourage us, and support us. Close friends transcend time and space. No matter what we have done or where we have been, they are always there for us. They overlook our faults and don't care about what we have. They care about us. Of all the people in your life, it is these few close friends who can speak into your life more than anyone else. No one knows you more than your closest friends. They understand you. They have witnessed you at your best and your worst, and you have witnessed them in the same circumstances. They have demonstrated their love and are among the few people you truly trust. They have your best in mind, and they know specifically how to speak to you and what to say to you when things need to be said.

Do you have a friend like that? Sometimes these friends come very easily. Usually, we need to nurture these friendships over the years. It is in our close friendships that we find accountability and support while traveling for work. This is one of the biggest mistakes I (Sam) made while traveling extensively. I did not include Wayne and others in my personal struggles along the way.

Another friend, Eric, developed a good system of accountability for when he travels. Here's an example of an e-mail message that he sent to his accountability team before a trip:

Hi Guys. Here are the details of my upcoming trip:

I arrive in Dallas on Tuesday at 5:45 p.m. CST on American Airlines. I'm staying at the airport Hilton. I have three appointments throughout the day on Wednesday and two on Thursday, one in the morning and one in the afternoon.

I anticipate being back at my hotel room by 7:00 p.m. Wednesday night where I will be doing some reading and praying, then getting to bed early. I will not be turning on the television at all.

My return flight will be on Thursday night and is scheduled to arrive into LAX by 8:00 p.m. PST.

Please cover me in prayer and I will see you guys on Friday morning for our weekly breakfast! I will check in with you if anything doesn't go according to this plan.

Thanks, Eric

We tend to think of our friends more as a source of fun and relationship than of formal accountability. But they are perfectly designed to be an ideal point of accountability.

Sometimes you develop a friendship with a person over the course of an entire lifetime. Sometimes you develop a friendship with a person at a certain job or when you go to a specific church. It is important that you work on developing some of these close friendships.

Perhaps you have had some close friends, but you have let time and space keep you from staying in touch. Perhaps you have some new friends but have been so busy you have not invested the time or felt the need to stay in touch. These relationships must be developed and nurtured to give you the right input and protection while you travel for work.

What defines a close friend? Close friends are the people you let into your personal life. They are the ones you feel comfortable sharing the "stuff" of your life with. Over time, you will expose more of the real you, and they will expose more of the real them. They will become intimately aware of who you are and how you operate, and you of them. The result is motivation to help each other because of the friendship. Trust gives you the ability to receive and give input into one another's lives.

How do you keep yourself accountable for your actions while you are on the road? Your close friends keep you accountable. Bottom line: these relationships must be invested in, as they provide an outlet for candid communication. Such communication includes providing details of the areas of temptation and challenge you face during travel. Accountability has a tremendously positive impact on protecting your personal life and relationships. Accountability keeps you in the light. Accountability is about maintaining a strong connection to the people in your life who know the real you (in addition to your spouse).

Accountability has three main components: support, visibility, and a plan. Let's address these three components of accountability in more detail.

1. Support

Support is all about staying in touch. In addition to your spouse, who should always be your first line of support, you should have a few close friends you stay in touch with while you're on the road. This process should feel effortless, with easy and open access to your friends readily available. Consistent, frequent communication should occur. This is the discipline of staying in touch and connected on how things are going, how you are feeling, and so on.

Isolation is one of the biggest barriers to growth. Isolation doesn't necessarily mean being alone. We can feel isolated when we are around a lot of the wrong people, people who are not connected with us at a deeper level and have no interest in our well-being. Isolation develops when we stop proactively spending time with the right people. It happens when we are not investing time with close friends. These people are motivated to invest time with us and will gladly and willingly support us.

Support starts with picking a few of your closest friends and asking them to keep you accountable while you are on the road. They should know and understand their role as part of your accountability team. Begin by asking your friends to just be available on a regular basis to meet and talk. This may seem obvious. You may think this is something you already do! But there's a good chance that as you have gotten busier and your travel schedule has become more intense, you have let times of close fellowship with friends slide. Sometimes these are the first relationships to be put on hold.

As you travel, you must intentionally stay connected. Your accountability friends should know that they have a special assignment to support you as you travel for work. You should have a routinely scheduled time to talk. This could be at a time when you or they are commuting on the road or at night. It could be in the morning. The key is that the appointment is made and kept.

2. Visibility

Visibility is all about direct questioning. Give your friends permission to ask you hard questions about anything. And offer information to them as well. We must learn to bring into the light the private conversations, fleeting thoughts, personal struggles, and personal interactions that occur while traveling for work. Once something is discussed and brought into the light, it loses its power to control you.

Questions might be as basic as:

- How are you doing with your travel?
- How are you doing with so much time alone?
- Is there anything you have faced the last few days that has been a struggle for you?
- Have you been tempted by anything?
- How are you doing with your spouse and kids?
- How can I support you and pray for you?

Being visible is a crucial component of protecting your personal life. It means you allow your close friends to see every aspect of your life. Friends in your accountability group may not be frequent travelers and may not understand the pressures of traveling. If that's the case, you'll need to be very candid about what you encounter when you're away from home.

Again, it is tremendously freeing to not have secrets. When you are visible, you are released from guilt, shame, and fear.

3. Plan

The third component of accountability with friends is a plan to put you on the offensive and ensure you prevent troubles before they occur. Establish a perimeter of protection around your life, and ask your friends to help you maintain it. You should create a battle plan and give your friends permission to ask you direct questions regarding how well you are following it.

This may seem like overkill, but it's not. Just remember how much is at stake. What you are dealing with will determine how big a plan you will need. Think of your plan as a battle strategy to protect your personal life and relationships. Have a complete script laid out in advance. Look at specific situations you have faced where you have struggled most. Create a scenario that defines exactly how you should respond. Work with a friend to create a script of what you would say and how you should respond in specific situations.

For example, how will you respond if someone flirts with you? How will you respond if you are confronted with a heavy-drinking environment? What will you say when someone asks you to do what you know you don't want to do or shouldn't do? How will you protect yourself inside your hotel room?

If you are not sure what you should do, just think about the situations you find yourself in when you're alone, then play out how you would act and respond if your spouse were sitting there with you.

Your battle plan must have built-in barriers that your friends can inspect and, if you need help, actually help you maintain. These include blocking channels in your hotel room, checking up on you late at night, calling you after dinner and asking where you are and who you are with, inspecting your PC and helping you maintain blocking software for e-mail and Web access. It might also include helping to keep you away from bars or other places you know you should stay clear of. Whenever you travel, e-mail your friends your travel itinerary with the scheduled times of appointments and all the specifics of when and where you will be.

Finally, set specific times to meet with your accountability team in person. Make these great times for all, with lots of good food and time for conversation. The best friends are those who are as interested in giving support as they are in receiving it. A good accountability group involves a free-flowing interchange of ideas with no boundaries on what can be shared. In addition to having a regularly scheduled time to meet, the accountability group should be one you can call together at a moment's notice if a need or issue arises.

The willingness to have people speak truth into your life is invaluable. Combined with a commitment to share truth and be open and honest, trusted friendships can lead to a life of fulfillment and consistent growth.

Questions to Ponder

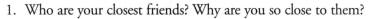

1. Who are your closest friends? Why are you so close to them?

2. How often do you stay in touch with each of them? What could you do to increase that time?

3. What would an accountability team look like to you in terms of meetings and other chances to talk about life? Who could be part of that team for you? (Note: these friends should be the same gender as you.)

14

Yourself for Balance

Your Personal Life Gives You Balance

- When you're driven, it's easy to put your own health at the bottom of your priority list. But if you're not healthy, everything else in your life will be out of sync. Balance is the key, and it begins with investing in your emotional, mental, spiritual, and physical health.
- How do you develop balance in your personal life while traveling for work? Balance requires intentionality. It doesn't just happen automatically. A balanced life requires you to:
    1. practice emotional health
    2. maintain physical health
    3. find and sustain favorite hobbies
    4. invest in your spiritual life

SAM'S JOURNAL ENTRY: PRESENT DAY

It is now 6:00 a.m. I start the coffee and splash water on my face. My first order of business today is to write my wife a love note of thanks. I want to let her know how thankful I am that she stuck with me for over twenty-five years. This will take a lifetime to really express, but each time I write, I learn something new about how I really feel about her.

I write, Toni, my love, this morning is full of new memories of you, and I can't wait to make more of them together. Your Sam. Each morning a new note, and each morning a new hug. Wow. I had no idea how much I needed to change on the inside.

When you're driven, it's easy to put your health at the bottom of your priority list. But if you're not healthy, everything else in your life will be out of sync. Balance is the key. Balance begins with investing in your emotional, mental, spiritual, and physical health. When you focus on maintaining a balanced life, you gain the right perspective from which to make healthy business-travel decisions. When you don't, it becomes nearly impossible to travel with the strength to keep your personal life and relationships intact.

We tend to think that the only visible sign of being out of balance is being overweight or out of shape. Yet if our emotions are not being properly fed, or if we've neglected time with the Lord, or if we've been filling our mind with too much junk, the result will be the same: a life out of balance. The fact is that all areas of life need to be developed.

How do you develop balance in your personal life while traveling for work?

Balance requires intentionality. It doesn't just happen automatically. The following are four components of a balanced life, and all are necessary when business travel is a part of your work routine.

PRACTICE EMOTIONAL HEALTH

Emotional health can be one of the hardest issues for men to buy into. We're not usually as in touch with our emotions as women are. Yet knowing how we feel and then responding appropriately according to those feelings is so important to living a balanced life. We can get so busy in the business of travel that we forget to maintain a healthy emotional state of being.

When it comes to emotional health, the rule of thumb is summarized in this simple yet complex maxim: *The funny thing about emotions is that they just want to be felt.*

It means that we can't stuff our emotions. Balance comes when we learn how to identify our emotions and what to do with them. They will not just go away if we stop dealing with them; they will build up over time.

What happens next is predictable, but it looks different for different people. We have to get our emotions out somehow—some of us develop stomach problems, some explode at the slightest provocations, others overeat in an effort to cope, and still others just lie on the couch all day long, unable to face the world.

These are some built-in warning signals that become visible when we aren't expressing our emotions properly. They tell us something is not right. If we spend the bulk of our time on the road out of balance, we tend to channel all our emotional energy into the wrong things, from depression to addictions. The results are the consequences that we looked at in the previous section of this book.

One of the keys to emotional health is an intentional decision to be grateful. First Thessalonians 5:18 instructs us to "give thanks in all circumstances."

This doesn't mean that you give thanks for bad circumstances, but rather in the circumstances or in spite of them. Gratefulness can be the overriding emotion through which other emotions are filtered.

And it is okay to have other emotions too. Jesus Christ demonstrated anger; He felt sorrow; He felt betrayed; He experienced joy.

A few chapters back, we talked about the dangers of not thinking, just doing. That principle can be applied to your emotional life as well. Sometimes it's very healthy to stop in the middle of an action or event and ask yourself what your emotion is at that particular moment. When you have identified what you're feeling, ask yourself why you're feeling that emotion. Then think of a way to appropriately express that feeling.

For example, perhaps you're at the airport and you catch yourself being rude to the man behind the check-in counter. Stop. Take a few moments to ask yourself what your emotion is and why it might be there.

- Are you *angry* because of slow or poor service?
- Are you *impatient* because you need to be somewhere on time?
- Are you *afraid* because you have an important meeting coming up?
- Are you *lonely* because you aren't connected to your family back home?

Now envision an appropriate outlet for that emotion. If service is indeed poor, maybe it means writing an e-mail of complaint to the airline. Maybe you need to call ahead and let your party know you're running behind schedule. Perhaps you need to review your notes for the upcoming meeting so you're better prepared. Maybe you need to call your wife and reconnect.

Sorting out your emotions isn't always easy. It takes time and intentionality, but it can be done. In fact, it *needs* to be done to maintain emotional health.

Another key to emotional health is to stay connected to those closest to you. Focus on each person in your inner circle, and remind yourself how much you care for that person. Let those thoughts fuel you to action.

An important ingredient of this kind of connection is a focus on giving love more than receiving it. While this focus might seem counterintuitive, it is one of the best ways to dismantle barriers to protection and health. Emotional health comes when you *serve* rather than *demand.*

If you're feeling emotionally out of balance, put your spouse first when you walk through the door each night. Next come your kids. Hang out with trusted friends. Whether words are spoken or not, just being with them will speak volumes and fulfill a place inside you.

MAINTAIN PHYSICAL HEALTH

This is one you know so well. Yet the tensions, travel schedules, and different time zones all make it difficult. The older we get, the more physical the toll that travel takes on the body.

We must factor our health into a travel schedule. While at home, exercise. Walk, run, lift—whatever you can do, just do it! While on the road, it is easier now more than ever to find hotels that offer exercise facilities. These are great alternatives to late-night bars. Instead of heading out for a drink, spend half an hour on a treadmill.

Diet is critical as well. In my earlier years of travel, I (Sam) did not focus much on diet and exercise. Before long I went from a healthy weight (for me) of 210 pounds to 248 pounds. At forty-two years I felt old, looked old, and had little energy and stamina. I've had to build a healthy diet and exercise back into my routine. There are many good books that can explain to you in detail how to do this. I'm now fifty and look younger, feel younger, and have more energy and stamina than I have had for years.

You must make your physical health a priority. There are a million excuses, but they are always flimsy. Don't have the time? Sure you do. You make time for that which is important to you.

FIND AND SUSTAIN FAVORITE HOBBIES

When you're driven, it's easy to think that all of life revolves around work. Or that life consists only of work. But we all need healthy activities that give us a fresh perspective on life. You don't have to spend *a lot* of time investing in things you really like to do. But you should invest *some* time.

Making time for hobbies can become easier if you invest in others first. Combine a hobby with a friend's or a family member's interest. Your family and friends will want to give back to you. Is your son really into video games? Why not try some out with him? Is your wife into antique shops? You may discover that you actually like what you find in them. Does your husband love golf, but it's not something you have experience with? Try taking some golf lessons so you can join him on the links.

It can be tough to develop a hobby if you aren't sure anymore what you enjoy doing. When was the last time you invested any time doing something you really liked to do? We have personal skills and abilities that must be developed in addition to our professional skills. What are your hobbies? What do you do to rest and recharge?

Hobbies have a way of coming back to help us in the end. They actually help improve business success. When we have a break from the intensities of work, we can sustain our careers longer. By investing in our personal life and health, we ensure we stay active in more than just work.

INVEST IN YOUR SPIRITUAL LIFE

In a previous chapter we spent a lot of time on the dimension of spiritual health. But it is important to discuss it a little more here.

Spiritual health is a part of you that sits idle until you engage it. In addition to reading God's Word, invest in books that will enhance your spiritual perspective on life. Good books can help bring you back to what's really important, as well as be a source of inspiration and hope.

Additionally, invest in prayer. Prayer is the way to connect with a source that is bigger than you. Every fear, concern, or point of need you have can be brought before the Lord in prayer. Or just talk with Him through the responsibilities and challenges of your day. The greatest source of strength and balance is waiting for you to talk to Him. He will give you answers to your unanswered questions; He will bring joy into your life as you stay in regular dialogue with Him. Don't worry about what you're going to say, just speak to God about what's on your mind and heart. Do this regularly and watch what happens.

YOUR PLAN TODAY

Sometimes a healthy lifestyle—emotional, physical, and spiritual—can seem like an unattainable goal, so we convince ourselves we're too far away and never make any progress toward it. We encourage you to invest in one thing at a time. Just do *something*. Do one thing today to help you on the road toward balance and health.

Too often we try to fix a symptom rather than heal the wound that's the source of a problem. If your dashboard light says the engine needs maintenance, the biggest mistake would be to fix the light. Instead, you need to fix something in the engine. Similarly it's a mistake to try to control addictions or other unhealthy behaviors without understanding their cause. Instead, we need to resolve painful emotions—such as guilt, shame, anger, rage, fear—that send our minds into negative and unhealthy places. When we heal these areas, then the compulsive behaviors can be brought under control.

When your life is balanced, you are in the right fame of mind for travel. And when you understand the principles of balance as a means of protection while you travel for work, you can travel more effectively. Balance helps you think clearly and gives you perspective from which to make good business-travel decisions. A healthy perspective provides the platform for protecting your personal life and relationships as you travel for work.

Questions to Ponder

1. What sources of anger, fear, or shame do you have that hurt your relationships with others? with yourself?
2. What could you do to work on replacing these with a life of peace? a life of purpose?
3. Which of the four areas is most out of balance in your life? What can you do to bring health and wholeness to it?

15

Just Say No

Take a Stand for Life

- Sometimes it's unavoidable to be away from home. Travel comes up, it's for legitimate reasons, and it's well within your responsibilities at home and work to be on the road. Yet one of the main premises of this book is that, as far as it depends on you, it's better to limit your time on the road and be connected to the key relationships in your life.

- "Just say no" was the simple message of an ad campaign that aired for several years, dealing directly with the deadly effects of drugs in the lives of children. Just saying no can be a powerful way to deal with the effects of extensive travel as well. So just say no to too much travel.

- When it comes to discretionary business traveling, three methods of establishing healthy boundaries include asking:
    1. your supervisor if a trip is absolutely necessary
    2. yourself who has control over this decision—you or the *trip*
    3. yourself if a key relationship needs immediate attention

Sometimes, it's unavoidable to be away from home. Travel comes up, it's for legitimate reasons, and it's well within your responsibilities at home and work to be on the road. Yet one of the premises of this book is that, as far as it depends on you, it's better to limit your time on the road and be connected to the key relationships in your life.

Two friends of mine (Sam) have been through medical crises with their children in recent years. Both friends travel. One was home when the crisis happened; one wasn't.

It's not always possible to be present, and I don't share these stories to heap guilt on you if you've been away from home when a crisis happened in your family's life. I share them, rather, to illustrate the power of simply being present.

Don writes:

At 7:00 a.m. my phone rang. I was out of town again. It was my wife. She was crying and sounded extremely frightened.

"Honey, I had to take Nick to the hospital early this morning. He had an allergic reaction to penicillin. It was awful. I didn't know what to do. I called my mom and dad and they came over. We rushed Nick to the emergency room. He couldn't breathe. He's okay now, but it was terrifying. I wish you were here. I needed you. We could have lost our son."

What could I do? I was three thousand miles away. That phrase my wife said has stayed with me for a long time: "I wish you were here."

Marty writes:

Around 10:30 p.m. I went to check on my three-year-old son, Brandon. Opening the door, I saw immediately that something was wrong. He was asleep, but his face was puffed up like a balloon. I yelled for my wife and we called 911.

Wrapping my son in my arms, I carried him out to the ambulance. He was barely breathing by then. I prayed over him as we raced to the hospital. My wife followed in our car.

When we got to the emergency room, it felt like the doctors took their time getting to him. Maybe this was wrong, I don't know, but I became this father bear, running around yelling, "My son needs help! My son needs help!"

A doctor appeared who knew exactly what to do. My son's life was saved from what turned out to be an infection.

My wife was a mess and cried throughout the whole ordeal. While we were waiting for a report from the doctor, my wife put her head on my shoulders and I held her tightly. All she could say was, "I'm glad you were here."

WHEN YOU MAKE A GOOD DECISION

An ad campaign that dealt directly with the deadly effects of drugs in the lives of children aired for several years. The message was simply, "Just say no." The idea was to stop an addiction before it started.

This tactic strikes me as a powerful way to deal with the effects of extensive travel as well. So just say no to too much travel.

Stopping the pursuit of loneliness is your responsibility. The way to do it is to consciously change the paradigm you use to decide whether or not to take each trip. Perhaps you're a long-haul trucker or an airline pilot. You have a set route that takes you away from home each week. Your invitation to "just say no" will look different from the one offered to a business professional who has more discretion on which trips he can take or not. If your job involves a predetermined amount of traveling, perhaps your decision to say no means you don't take extra work away from home. Perhaps it will mean switching shifts or routes so you spend more time at home. Perhaps, if your life is right on the brink of disaster, the healthiest thing you can do is to take a demotion or even quit your job for a season. In the long run, making a serious and difficult change will be better for you and your family than destroying your life.

At the core, saying no means you learn to set healthy boundaries with your employer when it comes to too much travel.

In the beginning, setting boundaries might feel foreign to you. It takes practice and wisdom to learn how to use the word *no* correctly. Your boss may not completely understand your reason for choosing to stay home instead of taking that next trip. You may have traveled so long that even your family expects you to go—they've all learned to deal with your being away most of the time. But you, and you alone, must break the pattern of loneliness and protect your personal life.

Let's look at some of the underlying paradigm shifts behind the decision to say no.

1. Ask if a Trip Is Absolutely Necessary

The first step to just saying no is learning to change why you decide to take a trip. Depending on the purpose of a trip, how long you need to be gone, and how broken things are in your personal life, you may need to say no to your next trip.

If you learn to say no early in your career and put a limit on the amount and timing of your trips, you can sustain a career that includes travel. But if you don't set boundaries on the frequency of your trips, the effects of loneliness may become too great to overcome.

You may be at a place where you need to stop traveling altogether. Sometimes you can make this decision yourself. Sometimes circumstances, your company, or trusted family members will need to make this decision for you.

If the decision is made for you, chances are it will be more painful. Likely it means that something has been wrong for too long. You have burned out.

If your company makes this decision for you, it will probably not be out of concern for your well-being. More likely, it will be because your performance does not meet the company's standards. This can be the most ironic part of the story. The company you have pursued professionally and have invested the most amount of time in may be where you find the least amount of loyalty in the end. Yet the place where you have invested the least amount of time (your family) is probably where the most loyalty toward you still exists.

We encourage you to not wait too long. Don't let someone make this decision for you.

2. Ask Who Has Control over This Decision

Sometimes your business has control over which trips you take. Travel is part of your job description or built into your contract.

Sometimes the *trip* will actually decide for you.

If that sounds strange, it is. When your trip decides, you have probably come to a place where travel has become an addiction for you. Travel has become a habit, compulsion, dependence, need, obsession, craving, or infatuation. Do any of those words define your business travel? If so, then it has taken control of your life. Your willpower means little at this point.

Part of knowing who has control over a decision depends on asking why a trip is necessary. For some, the request for travel becomes the only reason to travel. But please understand that you always have a choice. You regain control by admitting that extensive travel has become a business addiction. You have the power to say no. Sometimes trusted friends or family members will need to help you make this choice. But no job owns you. You can always walk away.

Never allow your decision to travel to rob you of all the nonrefundable personal moments that were created and designed just for you. No job is worth it.

Perhaps this sounds overly serious to you—calling business travel a potential addiction. But think about it. Even when everything seems fine, loneliness can build up in you beneath the surface. You must stop thinking that this is no big deal, that although you are married, you simply like being alone. Pornography is not harmless, flirting is not innocent, and those few drinks you have every night to help you sleep are not normal.

The harmful effects of too much travel are real. Some who travel may say they made it through, but most will say they have not. And frankly, no one makes it through years of business travel without some negative effects on them and their personal relationships.

This is what happened to me (Sam). From the outside I was a model dad, husband, and citizen. I was very active in the church we attended. I was involved in many things to keep me from getting too far off track. Then my work accelerated and I begin to experience significant business success, which (I thought) required significant travel. I used external filters for years, but I became too busy to keep up with them consistently. I believed I had enough willpower to keep clean. But as the rigors of the new job increased and my years of travel caught up with me, I fell when I least expected it.

Why? It was the cumulative effect of my pursuit of loneliness. Loneliness will overcome every external filter you put in place. Loneliness will drive you to do things you never thought you would do. You must address your pursuit of loneliness and become aware at a whole new level of what is happening to you every time you travel away from home. You must be aware that every time you say to yourself, "I am so lonely," your soul is giving you a verbal clue that you are pursuing loneliness. *It's time to just say no!*

3. Ask if a Key Relationship Needs Immediate Attention

What brings a person to the place of deep loneliness in the first place? We become lonely when our key relationships are neglected.

The hard part about figuring out if a relationship is neglected is that when you're home, problems can often be set aside. But as soon as you get on an airplane, the relationship suffers again.

The solution is to ask important questions of your five key personal relationships and then let them influence your travel decisions. If any one of your relationships—with God, your spouse, your children, your friends, or yourself—needs immediate attention, then you know you need to push back on the amount of time you're away. Let these relationships influence how much you can travel, when you can travel, and when you simply can't. When one or more of these relationships is not well cared for, you must say no to a requested trip.

Take a moment to think about how far these five key relationships are from being healthy right now. If *major* work is needed to heal a broken relationship, then you may need to take a break from business travel for a season. It will be necessary to restructure your business life to not include overnight trips. This could be extremely beneficial in the long run because it will allow you time to invest in the healing process.

Can you really do this? Yes, you can! How do I know? Because this is exactly what I (Sam) needed to do. At the peak of my career, I took a sideways step and spent the time necessary to reinvest in my most special and personal relationships. I never thought of it as doing something crazy. If my personal life and relationships are intact and flourishing, then my business career will flourish all the more. I needed to reorder how I managed my business life in the context of my personal life.

If you are in that place, then push the pause button on business travel for a while. How long you do so depends on you, but you will know when you can travel for work again. For me, it took one full year of not traveling at all. It took another five years after that to find the right balance between business travel and home life. Every trip was weighed through the criteria grid of deepening my five key relationships.

THE CHOICE IN FRONT OF YOU

The key to business travel is to intentionally manage every business travel request or directive you receive. Let your calendar reflect what you have learned!

There is no place in your life where the stakes are higher and no place where the damage is more permanent than in your personal relationships, and there is absolutely nothing you will regret more than the damage done to these relationships because of too much business travel. Simply put, success starts by scheduling more time at home.

Of all the things I (Steve) have written in this book, the most important to know is that there is hope. No matter where you are in your business travel life, you can start today building lasting, deep relationships that quell the pursuit of loneliness. Yet you must stop unchecked, unmanaged business travel.

Questions to Ponder

1. Are you willing to change your criteria for determining whether or not a trip is necessary? If so, share these with your spouse.
2. What will you change tomorrow based on what you have read in this book?
3. What types of changes do your spouse, kids, and friends think could be very helpful? If you don't know, talk to them about it. How willing are you to make some of these changes work?

16

Coming Home

The Process of Reentry

Quick Tips to Grab on the Go

- No matter how long you have been traveling extensively, there is a reentry process whenever you change your schedule and become more involved at home.
- Becoming reconnected is a process, not an event. It takes time to adjust to your family's daily life and schedules, and they with yours. In some cases, there is damage that must be addressed in the process.
- Give people space to work through issues in their own way.
- Broken relationships seldom heal instantly. Forgiveness can be a long and multiphased process.
- It's always tempting to return to "the familiar," even if the familiar was a place that brought harm to your life. Don't do it. Stay the course.

No matter how long you have been traveling extensively, there is a reentry process whenever you change your schedule and become more involved at home.

Becoming reconnected is a process, not an event. It takes time to adjust to your family's daily life and schedules, and they to yours. In some cases, there is damage that must be addressed in the process.

Knowing that an adjustment is a normal part of coming home will hopefully encourage you and help you prepare yourself to focus on the right things with the right attitudes. It is worth the investment of time and attention (and some pain) that you give to this process.

A friend of mine, Rob, recently made some changes to his travel schedule. He knows it is the right choice, but he hasn't found it easy. This is his story:

> After years of being out on the road, I am now home every night. I have successfully found another role in the company and am in the process of settling into the daily commute.
>
> I thought at first that everything would be fine and we'd be a family again. You know—I did my part. I made the sacrifice and left a position I was good at to be with my family. I could see burnout coming anyway, so I wasn't too upset at transitioning to the other position.
>
> But wow! I just have to ask myself, *What is going on?*
>
> All we seem to do now is fight. Nothing I do seems to make much difference, and I just seem to be in the way. My spouse doesn't seem to appreciate very much that I am home.
>
> This is a lot harder than I thought it would be. It's like starting over with her. Last week we were having an argument, and she even said, "I liked it better when you were away. Why don't you just go back on the road?"
>
> Ouch. Perhaps I made the wrong decision. Perhaps I need to get back on the road. I am not quite sure what to do now. I sure never expected this reaction.

ADDRESSING THE DAMAGE ON THE INSIDE

When something has been neglected for a long time, it requires an overhaul to get it working well again. I remember when I bought a twenty-year-old car with only seventeen thousand miles on it. When I looked at the car I thought. *This is going to be great! Look at the condition of this car. Not a scratch on it. Not a dent anywhere. It's still like new.*

But I didn't think about how much damage the car had incurred because it had not been driven very much all those years. All the seals in the engine had dried up. The tires were hard as rocks. The transmission needed a major service before it would work properly. The brakes, the wiper blades, the lights, the battery—all had to be fixed, replaced, or restored!

Relationships can be like that. On the outside, they look well maintained, but inside they're a mess. How much work is needed to restore your relationships will correspond to how much time you've spent away from them.

Getting back into the swing of things can take a few years. You must be patient. For every year you have been away, you have accumulated relationship "baggage" that must be unpacked. The baggage could be the result of simple neglect. It may be the result of more complex addictions. There may be moral failures that you or your spouse must process and work through when it comes time for forgiveness. Give each other the time you need. Know that every day is worth that investment.

The following are a few things to remember in the readjustment process.

ONE SIZE DOESN'T FIT ALL

Each member of your family is unique in how he or she will respond to your being home. One size does not fit all when it comes to how your spouse and children each feel, what they think about your being around all the time, how your absence has effected them, and what they need and want from you. One of your children might not miss a beat and just settle in to the fact you are now at the dinner table at night. Another child might require some time and space to adjust to your more frequent input into his or her life. Many things they do will have to be adjusted because of your new level of involvement. These will range from carpools to dinner and chores around the house. Homework schedules, television programs, and the things the kids have been allowed to do and not do while you have been away may change. Anything and everything is disrupted when you come home.

Before you changed your business travel schedule, your spouse made the bulk of the decisions around the house. Now you will exert you opinions and wishes. All of this is part of natural reentry process.

TRUST DOESN'T HAPPEN OVERNIGHT

Second, trust will need to be rebuilt. You may not feel you have been away long enough to need to rebuild trust with your spouse and children, but in most cases you will. The longer and more frequently you have traveled, the more of an issue trust will be for them. In each of your family member's minds, he or she has needed to process the reasons you were always away at critical times. If you have frequently missed things and not been at home during the moments of difficulty faced by various family members, trust will be something that will have to be repaired.

Time and circumstance will impact a person's ability to trust. If you, your spouse, and your children have experienced pain from past experiences that have been a result of your business travel schedule, trust will have to be rebuilt. This will take time, perhaps many years. While you may resent the need to reestablish trust, don't give up. Your consistent demonstration of your new behaviors will prevail. If you stay the course, trust will be renewed.

REPAIR TAKES TIME

Broken relationships seldom heal instantly. If you have failed in your relation-ships, chances are good that you've done things you regret. Repair is needed.

Whenever failure has happened, forgiveness will need to occur, and for-giveness can be a long and multiphased process. Give your spouse time and space to work through all the issues that need to be addressed in order to for-give you.

This might be a two-way street. Perhaps there are some things you may need to forgive your spouse for. You will need time and space to come to the place of forgiving him or her.

It's not easy to get to the place where a traveling spouse has to make nec-essary scheduling changes. It's also not easy to work through what needs to happen once that decision is made. The decision to travel less and be home more needs the support of a commitment to take the necessary time to allow forgiveness to do its work in relationships.

Forgiveness takes time, and it will happen in layers. Be aware of that, and do not give up. As you work through the issues together or with someone's help, it will be your commitment and love that help stay the course of reconciliation.

YOU MIGHT GET "THE SHAKES"

Withdrawal can happen when any addiction is being terminated. If you have been traveling extensively for years and finally stop, you will most likely expe-rience some symptoms of withdrawal. I call these the shakes.

The shakes are anything that disturbs your status quo. They are circum-stances that push you to a place of imbalance and require extreme measures to feel normal. For example, you have the shakes when you feel irritable, unable to do "nothing," as though you need to get up and leave, be productive, or just *do* something—but there's no longer a "fix" for these sensations.

For years you were constantly on the go. You found yourself someplace different each week. But now you are home. Nothing changes. It's a slower pace. Some things to consider when managing the shakes: find an area of your house to have some personal space. You'll need time to read and pray and sort things through. Then get involved in your children's events—all the sports or other activities they are involved in. If they are too old, get involved in something with your spouse that brings you into your community. Volunteer at your church or another good cause. Get involved in working seriously on your health.

The important thing is to focus your energy on your five key relationships. This focus is critical and will reduce your sense of withdrawal.

REMEMBER WHERE YOU CAME FROM

It's always tempting to want to return to the familiar, even if the familiar was the place that brought harm to your life.

Stay the course. Remember why you made these good changes—for all the right reasons. It is important that as the years go by you don't forget why you changed. Don't look back at what you gave up to be in this place. That can lead to resentment.

You made a great decision to come home. You did it! And one day you will look back and thank God you did what you did. You will see the fruit of changing the destructive path you were on. Remember why you made the change and never look back.

It is feasible that every part of living as a family will need to be relearned again, but know that it is possible and that it can work. If you commit—and continue to commit—to coming home, you will be amazed at the tremendous blessings that await you as you stay the course.

WELCOME HOME!

Humble willingness paves the way for healing and restoration. It paves the path toward forgiveness and seeking forgiveness. It seeks the best for others. It removes whatever is deteriorating and complicating relationships. It signs up to grow. It shows up to change. It looks for areas to serve. It laughs in the joy of experiencing a second chance.

Are you willing to make the necessary changes toward a life of balance and health?

Questions to Ponder

1. What are your three strongest desires or motives for adjusting your schedule to spend more time at home?
2. How can you adjust for travel "withdrawal" while at home? What types of activities can you do in order to get some alone time?
3. What can you do to help yourself with reentry? How can you help your family adjust to your new level of input at home? How about with your spouse specifically?

A Spouse's Perspective

Hope for Your Marriage at the Toughest of Times, by Toni Gallucci (Sam's Wife)

I wanted to share a story with you and address it specifically to spouses of frequent travelers who need more hope. This is a story I saw come true as Sam and I went through our very difficult time.

As you know, Sam traveled often over the course of the first twenty years of our marriage. Our relationship, especially over the last three years of his traveling, broke us down. All the time apart had caused big gaps to develop between us.

So when Sam shared his failures with me, I had so little emotion left, I didn't even cry. That's how dry I had gotten; I was empty and unemotional. Through the many years of living apart because of Sam's business travel, our lives had grown so distant that I wasn't surprised at all when the news came my way.

Many times during the previous years of his extensive business travel, I approached Sam in tears, wanting to change our lifestyle. As the years passed, however, and the travel still continued, I gave up all hope as to what I thought we could have together in our relationship. And so I settled myself into a relationship with Sam that was full of compromises. Sam had set work as his number one priority, and now we clearly saw the cost that we both incurred by choosing this priority.

At this point, I didn't trust Sam. He had failed me. The realities of how low our marriage had sunk blasted like a big horn. In my mind, the biggest hurdle was how I was ever going to trust Sam again. My lack of trust made it seem impossible for us to make progress toward resolution. This overwhelmed me. I didn't have a clue what to do. But what choice did I really have?

Well there *was* another choice.

I could have stayed on the same road I was on, although it had already proven to lead to hurt and destruction. But somehow I still took it into consideration. The Enemy was clearly in the midst of things and wanted to lead me further away from Sam and from God. This road would have led us both into more destruction and pain. That road would not only affect us but our children and future generations to come.

Could it be that this same force is trying to lead you into more destruction?

When you're weak, you need to make sure you're listening to the right voice, because a lot of crazy things will go through your head. In my lowest moments, my feelings were all over the place, and I couldn't think straight.

I needed God's help, so I brought it all before the Lord. This was the best thing I could have ever done, and because I asked, He gave me a clear reply. He told me that I didn't need to trust Sam (what a relief), *but I did need to trust Him*! This was a wake-up call for me to draw closer to God than ever before. I needed God to embrace me and hold me, to counsel me, to stroke me, to lift me up and build me up.

To me, this was a big leap of faith.

LEARNING TO TRUST AGAIN

I had to learn to trust Christ alone before I could ever learn to trust Sam again. I honestly thought I might die in the process. At the time it was like saying yes to falling off a cliff. Yet this was the first time in my life I really gave God something significant to fix... I gave Him all of me and all of Sam.

This act of giving it all to God wasn't easy, because it required me to hand over my control to Him. Actually, during this time, the Lord showed me several things in my own heart that also needed to change. He began showing me the hard places that had developed in my heart over the years. Although Sam was the one who had the major failure, both Sam and I needed God's help. I knew if our relationship was going to have any hope of survival, it would need to be God who did it. So I decided to let Him.

With all this in mind, Sam and I came together and recommitted our lives to Christ and each other. We agreed that this would mean doing things God's way and not our own. We were finally on the same page with a plan we both agreed to, and in this I started to see there was hope! The Lord used His Word to minister to me in a way I had never experienced before. God started building me up and strengthening me, and I gained a new excitement about my relationship with Him. Since both Sam and I had allowed God to take the rubble that was left in our relationship, He started rebuilding it for us.

WHEN RUBBLE GETS REBUILT

It is amazing that though the Bible was written so long ago, God wrote it for us to read now in our time. Just as He wrote it for Sam and me, He also wrote it for you and your spouse.

Some of you reading this chapter may feel there is no hope left. Too much time has been spent on the road away from home, too much has happened over the years, and the result is that you have no hope for your marriage. While it is beyond the scope of this book to answer every need you have to put your marriage back together, I have to share with you that Sam and I are living proof of the Lord's miraculous ability to take a relationship that was completely dry, numb, unfulfilling, and based solely on commitment, and then *change* it and *restore* it. And, best of all, as a wife…satisfy me!

This is the good news of Jesus in action that I bring to give you hope! It can be your hope too, if you draw near to the Lord during this time, as both Sam and I did. After all the years Sam traveled apart from me, we are finally traveling on the same road, learning together and traveling together with Him. The Lord is willing and able to help you in your marriage today.

God is a God of restoration. That's why He came to the earth. He was willing to die for us to bring you and me to life. If He can raise the dead, you bet He can definitely restore a marriage. If He could create this world out of nothing, He can also restore and create a beautiful relationship for you both.

There is great hope when we finally decide to place our hope entirely in Him. When we place our hope in Him, we receive divine help from Him. He died so that we could receive His gift of life. And now we have the privilege of walking with Him through this life together.

Because God loves you and your spouse so much, He doesn't want your marriage to be dry and unfulfilling. He doesn't want you to have a marriage full of frustration and emptiness. The truth is that none of us want this. So what does He do? He puts the realities of your relationship in front of you both (as if constantly looking into a mirror), so that you can see it all so clearly, and so that it's not hidden from you anymore—everything is now all in the open. This can be painful, but it is necessary. We need to see exactly what's ailing us so we can get treatment.

Why does God show you these hard truths? There's good news in the answer to this question: because He wants you both to have so much more! God was sick of watching Sam and me get ripped off, and He feels the same way about you. He has given you so much, but the Enemy has gotten in and is robbing you of all of it—weakening you both tremendously. God has had enough of this, so He's stepping in to show you the hard realities that you have allowed into your marriage. He wants to rescue you and remove all the garbage. God wants to help you both fight this battle. When you allow Him to step in, He will help you win!

Ecclesiastes 4:12 tells us "a three-stranded rope isn't easily snapped" (MSG). That's you, your spouse, and the Lord.

Your willingness is required in this process. It's not fair to cry, "Save me, Lord!" and continue to develop and fuel bitterness, anger, jealousy, resentment, and hatred in your relationship. Don't act on these feelings alone, but use them to find the root issues and attempt to deal with them before making any long-term decisions.

Let God Himself step in, as we did. He is waiting for you two to make your choice, and know that it's a *major* choice. I remember the Lord asking me as He is now asking you: *Do you really believe Me? Will you really trust Me? Will you trust Me in this marriage? Will you let My Word guide you in this dark and confusing time? Or will you let your feelings and eyes guide you?* These are heavy questions, but ones we must all answer if we desire change in our lives.

My kids know what Sam and I went through. They also know Sam's entire story. But my kids know and have seen what God is able to do when we decide to do things His way. Through this process, my kids have grown in their faith, and the Lord is blessing our choices. I get emotional when I think back to the time the Enemy had me cornered. I could have chosen the path of least resistance. But in this scenario, my kids would never have gotten to see the amazing works of the Lord. His ability to truly rescue and redeem and restore would have been missed. We would have missed seeing a miracle together, and our family would have been forever fragmented. Satan has come "only to steal and kill and destroy," but don't let him have any more ground in your life or your marriage (John 10:10). Refuse to tolerate him any longer.

Let God take your feet out of the snare Satan has you in and start you on your journey to recovery. You will be amazed as you will get to personally experience God's hands tending each and every one of your deep wounds. You will witness Him and be amazed.

With love and great hope,

Toni

Visit the road warrior community at
www.ARoadWarriorsGuide.com.

The best-selling every man series,
coauthored by Stephen Arterburn,
provides resources for men in hot pursuit
of God's best in every area of life.

Every Man's Battle

Every Man's Marriage

Every Young Man's Battle

Every Man's Challenge

Every Man, God's Man

Preparing Your Son for Every Man's Battle

Every Heart Restored

Every Day for Every Man

Every Single Man's Battle

Every Young Man, God's Man

2.5 MILLION COPIES SOLD IN THE SERIES!

Available in bookstores and from online retailers.

WATERBROOK PRESS
www.waterbrookpress.com

New Life Ministries

Building Character
and Transforming Lives
Through God's Truth

New Life Ministries is a non profit organization, founded by author and speaker, Stephen Arterburn. Our mission is to identify and compassionately respond to the needs of those seeking healing and restoration through God's truth.

New Life's ministry of healing and transformation includes:

- *New Life* – our daily, call-in counseling radio program hosted by Stephen Arterburn. To find a station near you call 1-800-NEW-LIFE or go to www.newlife.com. You can also listen online.
- *Counselors* – our network of over 700 counselors nationwide. Call 1-800-NEW-LIFE to find one near you.
- *Weekend Intensive Workshops and Seminars*
  - *Every Man's Battle*
  - *Healing Is a Choice*
  - *Lose It for Life*
  - *Nights of Healing*
- *Coaching* – Our personal coaching program is "Professional Accountability" to come alongside you and give you solution-focused direction.
- *Website*
  - Podcasts and broadcasts of *New Life*
  - Blogs, message boards and chats
  - Our online store, featuring products by our radio show hosts
  - Find workshops and counselors in your area
- *24-Hour Call Center* – There is someone answering calls in our Call Center, 24 hours a day, 7 days a week, 365 days a year.

1-800-New-Life   www.newlife.com